M000114466

I Like Big Buts

REFLECTIONS ON PAUL'S LETTER TO THE ROMANS

Jason Micheli
Taylor Mertins
Teer Hardy
&
Johanna Hartelius

Copyright © Jason Micheli, Taylor Mertins, Teer Hardy, and Johanna
Hartelius

Unless otherwise noted, the Scripture quotations are from New Revised
Standard Version Bible, copyright © 1989 National Council of the
Churches of Christ in the United States of America. Used by
permission. All rights reserved.

"**_But now_**, apart from the law, the righteousness of God has been disclosed through faith in Jesus Christ.."

Romans 3.21

"The Reformation was a time when men went blind, staggering drunk because they had discovered, in the dusty basement of late medievalism, a whole cellar full of fifteen-hundred-year-old, two-hundred proof Grace–bottle after bottle of pure distilate of Scripture, one sip of which would convince anyone that God saves us single-handedly."

Robert Capon, *Between Noon and Three*

Table of Contents

Meet the Team

Crackers and Grape Juice began in the spring of 2016 with a conversation between Jason Micheli and Teer Hardy. In the years since, two shows have been added to the podcast lineup, Strangely Warmed and (Her)Men*You*Tics, but the goal has remained the same: talking about faith without using stained-glass language.

Jason Micheli is a United Methodist pastor in Annandale, Virginia, having earned degrees from the University of Virginia and Princeton Theological Seminary. He writes the Tamed Cynic blog (tamedcynic.org) and is the author Cancer is Funny: Keeping Faith in Stage Serious Chemo. He lives in the Washington, DC, area with his wife and two sons.

Teer Hardy is husband, father, and brewery theologian. He lives in Arlington, Virginia and is a United Methodist Pastor. Teer has received degrees from West Virginia Wesleyan College and Wesley Theological Seminary. Keep up with his sermons and thoughts on his blog (teerhardy.com) or on Twitter @teerhardy.

Taylor Mertins is a United Methodist pastor in Woodbridge, Virginia, having earned degrees from James Madison University and Duke Divinity School. He regularly posts sermons, devotionals, and other theological reflections at his blog (ThinkandLetThink.com) and you can follow him on Twitter @tcmertins. Taylor is the host of Strangely Warmed.

Dr. Johanna Hartelius is a message expert and founder of VDF Consulting and Professor of Rhetoric at the University of Texas, Austin. She works with clients at all stages from conceptual invention of ideas and products to the creation of audience strategies. With extensive experience as a professor and award-winning scholar, she leverages her expertise to assess and develop clients' internal communication as well as public image. Johanna is the host of (Her)men•you•tics.

Introduction

Dr. Johanna Hartelius

Having neglected Bible study for twenty years, I am one of those Christians who has returned to the New Testament in my late thirties. At this stage of life, I am confronted as we all are by the "What does it all mean?" question. Which is almost always followed by the even more unsettling "What am I supposed to do?" And as I read through the gospels into the letters, I have that cliché realization: "Wow, Paul was really onto something!" Paul, as you'll quickly discover through the ancient wisdom of Wikipedia, was a prolific writer and a brilliant theologian.

In the present tense, he speaks courageously about the world we live in and the life that we have been promised, never keeping his own sin a secret, or withholding the glory of God. Moreover, as I writer myself, I can appreciate how Paul goes right for the proselytic gold. A letter to Rome wasn't just a letter to some backwater town; nor was the contents of his writing simple pleasantries. Or even tips and life-hacks for the house-church of Roman Christians. Paul was writing dangerous things to a city where very powerful people lived. This is only one of the things I dig about him, and the Roman epistle specifically. I also like the substance and poetics of his announcement of salvation. It is in Romans that Paul proclaims that through the death that Jesus Christ died, he died to sin once for all; but that the life he lives, he lives to God (6:10).

It is in Romans that Paul reveals that he is convinced that neither death nor life nor angels nor demons nor the present or future—really not anything or any power in all of creation—can separate us from the love of God that is in Christ Jesus (8:38). And even pithier—I love this one especially—Paul assures us in Romans that, if God is for us, who could be against us? (8:31).

In the sermons that follow my introduction, you'll find three United Methodist pastors doing what pastors do, sharing the good news. And trying to help us members of the laity get a healthy dose of some blessed catechism.

Many of the sermons in this collection are Jason's, so they can't all be winners. The first one is exceptionally insightful, and starts the book off on just the right note. Definitely earmark that one for careful reading. The second one is mostly about how Jason wishes he were Billy Chrystal, which I think we can all agree is a pipe-dream. Jason would never think there was "too much pepper" on his paprikash. Then in the sermon regrettably titled "Junk in the Trunk," Jason addresses one of the most important and sublimely beautiful and terrifying points of the whole epistle: That not one of us humans is righteous. That's not what righteous means; righteous means something else, and Paul cover that, too. But the message is this: We are all "those people," even the obnoxiously "perfect" friends/neighbors/Christians/supermoms. Because we are human, we are all imperfect AND, not but, it's ok. We are forgiven. We are restored to love. On page 30, though, Jason forgets about the "don't judge others" part. Don't miss it. It's the only place in the book where Jason recognizes that he might not know everything.

Taylor, in his sermon on open hearts, minds, and doors, takes us directly to the promise of God and the salvation of faith as Paul proclaims it in Romans 4. The verse that stands out in the passage is a favorite: "If it is the adherents of the law who are to be the heirs, faith is null and the promise is void." If, like me, you never went to seminary, you may read this verse with some questions: Who are the "adherents of the law," exactly? (And here you start to get anxious that the answer could possibly be vaguely anti-Semitic. It's not. Paul was a super-Jew. But lots of good things get used for crappy ends, including and especially Scripture.) Second, heirs to what? Third, I thought I had faith – Is there a chance that my faith-check and the promise of God's stamp on it could be made null and void?! That sounds terrible! How can I make sure that doesn't happen?! Taylor, like a loving preacher should, takes us patiently through the long passage, hearing our tacit questions, and speaking to them. The most explicit and accessible message he offers is: If you want to do good things, make the church that you call home a place where no one is alone. That's a solid sermon take-home, and something we should indeed strive for. For my money, however, Taylor's most subtle point in the sermon is that faith, the substance that keeps a Christian community together, is a gift from God. It is less a characteristic of an individual than an active being-with God in which God, not the individual, is in control. As I explicate this, I'm not trying to take over Taylor's sermon so much as I am reflecting his analysis from another angle: Perhaps instead of making sure the pews are full, and full of people with just the right attitudes, and instead of spending endless time using the latest buzzwords in the right way, just trust that God is doing the Thing. He's got it. He runs the Church. Only He has accomplished—better yet, is effecting in the event of always-now—what is meant by dying for us while we were still sinners, which Taylor returns to in "The Elephant in the Room."

Teer's sermon "The Wedding Jacket" is a delightful surprise. Because Teer is one of those pastors whose lack of ego-investment makes them barely own the word pastor, I didn't expect such a hefty theological treatment. (You might say on this subject that Teer and Jason have "different approaches" to preaching. One has a lot of ego-investment. I won't say who…) Second, Teer's sermon begins with about eleven pages on the National Basketball Association (not quite, but almost). And just when I was about to doze off, he suddenly busts into a rich treatment of the life that Christians are called to live, not so that we can earn God's forgiveness and salvation, but because we are already loved. We are at peace, which isn't like the cucumber scented peace of a bathrobe spa, but like the peace of a cosmic adjustment toward rightness. We already have the wedding jackets. What we are called to do, Teer explains through Paul's parable, is wear them. And be in the world, the scary and violent and suffering world, without fear. Because, if God is for us, who could be against us?

The subjects of the sermons included here vary widely from a pregnant teenager to Bernie Sanders and revolutionary ambitions in small-town Virginia. And all three of the preachers deftly speak the vernacular of their homological moment. That is, all three of them thoughtfully combine Scripture with pop culture references and a certain self-deprecating tone that resonates with their audiences. That tone is effortlessly familiar. We are all used to hearing and reading media messages that assure the audience of the speaker's or writer's coolness. In short, it is clear that Jason, Taylor, and Teer have all to some degree mastered rhetorical cool. And that may be something that you're sick of. I get it. And yet, you may want to give them the benefit of the doubt. The themes that recur through the sermons of this collection are undeniable and perennially important: What is sin, and how do we summon the courage to talk about it? Can reasonable twenty-first century Americans live a life of faith for real if that life means trusting in something completely impossible? How do we help people live with love and kindness while eradicating the blight of self-righteousness? And what on earth are we supposed to spend our time on when, on one hand, we know that God has already saved the world, yet, on the other hand, absolutely everything is going to Hell in a handbasket and all we can do is Instagram pictures of food?

It really is no wonder that we, myself included, turn to Christian teachers like Teer and Taylor and even Jason for comfort in all the devastation.

When you've finished reading Jason's and Taylor's and Teer's sermons, I invite you to go and dig out your own Bible—or, let's be serious, go online and find Paul's letters to the Romans. Remind yourself that, when you read, you're going to try to think both about who Paul really was far away in the distant past, and how his words of grace and salvation are great news (gospel, in fact) for you in this very moment! Think about his itinerant life in the hot sun, sometimes making good headway and sometimes struggling with doubt and fearing for his safety.

As you start reading, you'll discover that, like any good letter-writer, Paul starts out talking about himself. He does that a lot, explaining where he is in the region and what's next on his agenda. Then he pats the Roman Christians on the back for doing an ok job at life. And then —and this is a big deal in Jason's first sermon, where he explains how the gospel reveals the active rectifying that God does—he announces that despite who he is and his family's heritage, Paul is not ashamed of the gospel. The gospel, he explains, is powerful; and because he uses the word dúnamis, we might paraphrase Paul as saying that he's not ashamed to love the gospel of Jesus Christ because the gospel's got good juice in it. The way someone might say that the Hadron particle collider of the CERN laboratories has good juice in it. Then think about that, and what it feels like to be enveloped and restored to God by that power. That all-exceeding force and intensity of love.

And I'm sorry about the title of the book. I was not consulted.

May the peace of God which passes all understanding be upon you and remain with you always.

- Johanna

Romans 1:16-17 - Immortal Combat

Jason Micheli

Ascension Sunday

For I am not ashamed of the gospel; it is the power of God for salvation to everyone who has faith, to the Jew first and also to the Greek. For in it the righteousness of God is revealed through faith for faith; as it is written, "The one who is righteous will live by faith."

- Romans 1.16-17

You probably saw the story in the *Washington Post* this week. I blogged about it too—as it turned out an unwise move that netted me 73 colorful comments from all over the interwebs, most of which contained too many four-letter words to publish.

I didn't know they had emojis for some of the acts critics suggested I do to myself.

You probably saw the article about how the Alexandria chapter of Washington Sport and Health this week cancelled the gym membership of Richard Spencer, the president of the Alt-Right/White Nationalist "National Policy Institute."

Spencer was pumping iron in safe anonymity, when C. Christine Fair, a Georgetown University Professor, recognized him and then confronted him. At first he denied his identity. But she was sure it was him. According to the other patrons, the professor lambasted him, yelling:

"Not only are you a Nazi—you are a cowardly Nazi... I just want to say to you, I'm sick of your crap—that this country belongs [to people like you]. . . . As a woman, I find your statements to be particularly odious; moreover."

The gym cancelled his membership after the altercation.

I doubt Richard Spencer was surprised at getting the heave-ho. The episode this week was only the latest in a string of ugly confrontations.

He was punched in the face on Inauguration Day by an anti-Trump protestor.

The chocolate shop on King Street near Spencer's rented town house went bust after boycotters assumed both spaces shared the same owner.

Before he was working out at the gym this week, Spencer was leading a march of demonstrators in Charlottesville, protesting the removal of a statue of Robert E. Lee.

Perhaps it's because we're kicking-off a summer-long sermon series on Paul's Letter to the Romans—the most important book of the New Testament—but reading the <u>article</u> in the *Washington Post* this week, my first thought was:

"That's what makes the Church different than the gym."

I don't know Dr. Fair, the Georgetown professor, and I wouldn't disagree with her characterization of Richard Spencer as a repugnant, cowardly Nazi. I'd even go farther than her. I don't know Dr. Fair but —if she's a Christian—rather than agitate for his removal from a club her first response to Richard Spencer should have been to invite him to the club we call Church.

————

Now, hear me out. I'm NOT suggesting Richard Spencer is entitled to whatever beliefs he wishes to hold.

I'm a Christian. I don't believe we're entitled to whatever beliefs we wish to believe. After all, today is the holy day we call Ascension, when the creeds shift from the past perfect tense to the present tense. Jesus *sits* at the right hand of the Father who has given Jesus dominion over all the Earth.

Because of Ascension, because Jesus is Lord and King over all the Earth, it now makes no sense whatsoever for us to say "As a Christian, I believe _____, but that's just my personal belief." The language of personal beliefs and private faith is unintelligible in light of the Ascension.

Jesus is Lord—that's a public, all-encompassing claim so, no, we're not entitled to believe whatever we wish to believe. We're required not only to believe *in* Jesus but to *believe Jesus*, believe what Jesus says and does, and what Richard Spencer believes grossly contradicts much of what Jesus says and does.

I'm not suggesting Richard Spencer is entitled to his noxious views nor am I minimizing the sort of person Richard Spencer appears to be in public.

By all accounts Richard Spencer's awful hipster side-part comes accompanied by monstrosity.

He's racist. He's anti-Semitic. He's xenophobic. He's an America First nationalist, which—by the way—is idolatry. Given that string, he's likely homophobic and sexist to boot.

During the campaign he provoked audible revulsion in the *NPR* reporter who was interviewing him. *The Atlantic* posted video of him leading a conference room full of disciples in the Sieg Heil salute.

In response to getting booted from Washington Sport and Health, Spencer tweeted: [Does this mean] "we can start kicking Jews and coloreds out of our business establishments?"

He has a knack for inducing revulsion.

I can think of no one who fits the definition better:

Richard Spencer is ungodly.

And that's my problem—and your problem.

Because the Apostle Paul says it's exactly someone like Richard Spencer for whom Christ died (Romans 5:6).

————

Obviously private gyms can do whatever they wish. And if it was a gym to which we all belonged then I'd be the first to say kick him out on his a@#.

But we're not members of a club. We're members of a Body, a Body created by a particular *kerygma*, a particular proclamation—the Gospel proclamation that on the law-cursed cross God in Jesus Christ died for the ungodly and that that death defeated the Power of Death.

Christ didn't die to confer blessings upon good people like you. Christ didn't die to make nice people nicer. Christ died so that ungodly people might become a new humanity. Richard Spencer is precisely the sort of ungodly person we should invite to Church.

Where else could he go?

This is the only place.

This is the only place where the Word of the Cross might vanquish him, delivering him from his bondage to the Power of Sin.

13

I chose that last sentence with care:

"Bondage to the Power of Sin," with a capital P and a capital S, is the only way to speak Christianly about Richard Spencer's racism; in fact, the Power of Sin with a capital P and a capital S is the only way to speak Christian.

————

Despite what you may think, the letters of Paul are not secondary to the Gospels, they are the means by which we read the Gospels, for the Gospels are not self-interpreting nor is their meaning self-evident.

No matter how your New Testament is ordered, Paul's *Gospel message* predates *the Gospels* (Matthew, Mark, Luke, and John).

"For I am not ashamed of the gospel; it is the power of God for salvation to everyone who has faith, to the Jew first and also to the Greek. For in it the righteousness of God is revealed through faith for faith; as it is written, 'The one who is righteous will live by faith'" (1:16-17).

This is Paul's thesis statement and from it he unwinds a single, long, nonlinear argument. The argument itself is odd.

Like Paul's other letters this one is addressed to a particular people, but unlike Paul's other letters this one continuously shifts focus from the congregation to the cosmic, that what concerns this little house church in Rome somehow also concerns all of creation.

The letter is also odd in that Paul sticks the salutations along with the introduction of the main theme not at the beginning of the letter but at the very end. The introduction of the main theme doesn't come until the very end of the letter, like a final, it's-all-been-building-to-this reveal:

"The God of peace will in due time crush the Power of Satan under your feet" (16.20).

This whole letter, all 16 chapters of it, all the pretty parts we like to read at funerals and to stick onto Hallmark cards, all of it is driving towards this: **"The God of peace will in due time crush the Power of Satan under your feet."**

This whole letter is about the defeat of the Power of Satan.

That's why throughout Romans Paul's focus keeps shifting from the congregational to the cosmic and why the language he most often uses is martial language, the language of combat and battle and powers and invasion (4.25, 8.32 et al).

The theme of this whole letter is the defeat of the Power of Satan, and Paul's thesis here in Romans 1 is that the Gospel is the Power by which God defeats that Power:

"For I am not ashamed of the gospel...For in it the righteousness of God is revealed..."

————

Trouble is—

Paul's thesis statement doesn't much sound like it's about the defeat of anything, much less the Power of Satan.

That's because the English language lacks any equivalents to the Greek word Paul uses here, the word that gets translated throughout Romans as either "righteousness" or "justification."

It's the same word: *dikaiosyne*.

When it gets translated as "righteousness" we hear it as an attribute or adjective of God, as God's holiness or perfection—the arrival of which to us doesn't sound like it would be good news.

When it gets translated as "justification" we hear it as our acquittal, as God declaring us something we're not: justified.

Neither is correct, and the problem is with the English translation. In the Greek, *dikaiosyne* is a noun with the force of a verb; it creates that which it names.

The only word in English that comes close to approximating *dikaiosyne* is rectify or rectification.

So "righteousness" here in Romans 1 isn't an attribute or adjective. It's a Power. It's a Power to bring salvation to pass. It's God's powerful activity to make right—to rectify—what is wrong in the world.

To say that God is righteous is to say that God is at work to make right.

And the way God is at work in the world, rectifying what is wrong in the world, is the Gospel, the Word of the Cross. Through it, God's rectifying power is *revealed*.

That word *revealed*—in Greek it's *apokaluptetai: Apocalypse. Invasion.*

Literally, Paul says: **"For I am not ashamed of the Gospel for in it the rectifying power of God is invading…"**

Note the present tense.

"For I am not ashamed of the Gospel for in it the rectifying power of God is invading…"

You can only invade territory held by an enemy.

The language of invasion is the language of liberation.

For as much as we think Christianity is about forgiveness, the Gospel of John uses the word forgiveness only once and Paul never does—nor does he use the word "repent."

Repenting is something *we* do.

Paul's Letter to the Romans isn't at all about anything we do. It's everywhere about what *God* does.

It makes no sense to forgive slaves for their enslavement. Captives cannot repent their way out of bondage. Prisoners can only be freed. Liberated. Delivered.

You see—if you think of sin as something you do, then you cannot understand what the Son of God came to do.

Only at the end of his long letter does Paul finally reveal the Enemy as Satan.

In chapter 3 he names the enemy Sin with a capital S and calls it an alien, anti-god Power whose power we are all under and from whom not one of us is able through our own agency to free ourselves (3:9).

In chapter 5 he make Sin-with-a-capital-S synonymous with Death-with-a-capital-D (5:12).

In chapter 8 he identifies the forms that the Power of Sin and Death take in our world to contend against us (8:35, 38) then he widens the lens to show how it's not just us but all of creation that is held in captivity to the Power of Sin and Death (8:21).

And in chapter 13 he tells the Christians in Rome that they should put away the works of darkness and put on the "weapons of light" (13:12), which 7 chapters earlier he calls the "weapons of rectification" (6.13).

Then, finally at the end, he reveals the Enemy as the Power of Satan.

Cliff-Notes Takeaway:

Only the faithfulness of Christ unto the cross is able to rectify what the Power of Sin has broken in God's creation.

And only the power of this Gospel can free us from our bonds to a Power that doesn't yet know it's been defeated.

———

Outside the Church this weekend it's Memorial Day, when we remember those who've fallen in war.

But inside the Church we've not remembered.

We've forgotten that salvation itself is a battle. We've forgotten, such that this all probably sounds strange to you.

We've forgotten that God has a real Enemy God is determined to destroy (1 Cor 15:24–26).

We've forgotten that the cross of Jesus Christ is God's invasion from on high and that our proclamation of his act upon the cross is itself the weapon by which the God of peace is even now rectifying a world where Satan still rules—but his defeat is not in question.

We've forgotten that the language of salvation is itself the language of war.

Salvation isn't about individuals going to heaven when they die. Salvation is cosmic because all of creation is in captivity to the Power of Sin, the Power of Death—the Power of Satan, whom Paul finally names at the end of his letter.

Salvation isn't our evacuation from earth to God.

Salvation is God's invasion of earth in and through the cross of Jesus Christ, the Power that looks like no power.

Only when you understand scripture's view of Sin as a Power and our sinfulness as bondage to it can you understand why and how Paul can claim something as repugnant as there being no distinction whatsoever between someone like you and someone like Richard Spencer (2:1).

That's not to say you're all as awful as Richard Spencer; it's to say that all of us are captive, because all of creation is captive.

17

We're all captives to a Pharaoh called Sin, which is to say, we're all ungodly (5:10).

And not one of us is safe from God's rectifying work.

To invite Richard Spencer to Church then isn't to minimize or dismiss his noxious racism or odious views.

It's to take them so seriously that you invite him to the only place where he might by assaulted by the only Word with the Power to vanquish him and create him anew.

Or, to put it Paul's way plainer:

"I am not ashamed of the gospel; it is the power of God for salvation to everyone who has faith, to the Jew first and also to the Greek.

For in the Gospel the rectifying work of God is invading the world through the faithfulness of Jesus Christ who was obedient all the way to the cross, a faithfulness which has power to create faith...'"

"[A Power]...that will in due time crush the Power of Satan under *your* feet."

———

During their confrontation at Washington Sport and Health, Dr. Fair, the Georgetown Professor, yelled at Richard Spencer: "I find your presence in this gym to be unacceptable, your presence in this town to be unacceptable."

The gym later terminated his membership without comment.

In all likelihood inviting him to church would be as bad for our business as the management of the gym judged it to be bad for their business.

But maybe "bad for business" is what Paul means by the scandal of the Gospel.

You haven't really digested the offense of the Gospel until you've swallowed the realization it means someone like Richard Spencer might be sitting in the pew next to you, his hand out to pass the peace of Christ, the weapon which surpasses all understanding.

You haven't really comprehended the cosmic scope of God's salvation until you realized it includes both you and Richard Spencer, both of you potential victims of the awful invading power of the Gospel of God's unconditional grace.

I haven't actually invited Richard Spencer to this church.

Yet.

But I did leave a copy of this sermon in the door of his townhouse yesterday.

I don't know that he'd ever show up.

But I do know—I'm not ashamed of it—I do know that this Gospel is powerful enough to defeat the Powers of the Enemy that enslaves him.

Romans 3:1-8 Circumcision is Physical?
Teer Hardy

*Then what advantage has the Jew? Or what is the value of
circumcision? 2 Much, in every way. For in the first place the Jews[a] were
entrusted with the oracles of God. 3 What if some were unfaithful? Will their
faithlessness nullify the faithfulness of God? 4 By no means! Although
everyone is a liar, let God be proved true, as it is written, "So that you may be
justified in your words, and prevail in your judging."[b] 5 But if our injustice
serves to confirm the justice of God, what should we say? That God is unjust
to inflict wrath on us? (I speak in a human way.) 6 By no means! For then how
could God judge the world? 7 But if through my falsehood God's truthfulness
abounds to his glory, why am I still being condemned as a sinner? 8 And why
not say (as some people slander us by saying that we say), "Let us do evil so
that good may come"? Their condemnation is deserved!*

-Romans 3:1-18

I asked Jason in his office this week, "What does Paul mean
circumcision is not physical? Jason being ever appropriate and full of
reverence responded by say, "We have 15 boys in our confirmation
class this year, I think that they, you, and I would agree that
circumcision is about as physical as it gets!"

When I first arrived on campus at Wesley Theological Seminary I was
forced to enter into a covenant. As part of a class titled 'Spiritual
Formation for the Practice of Ministry,' a class I cynically referred to as
my 3 hour weekly waste of time in DC, I entered into a covenant with
six other first year seminary students. I could not have made up the
makeup of this group.

There was Chris, an Army computer analyst who pushed back at
everything our professor said.

Okey, an Air Force Chaplain candidate who was glued to his phone.

Sharon, the director of religion and faith programs at the Human Rights
Campaign.

Melvin a licensed local pastor from Baltimore who was more longwinded than Jason.

Monica a stay at home mom who really needed to cut back on her caffeine intake.

Then there was me, the State Department contractor who was just there to get his class credit and move on.

These were people that I would have never hung out with outside of class. But here we were, assigned to the same group for the rest of the year. We covenanted to pray for one another, serve the community with one another, and help carry one another through our first year in seminary.

The "touchy-feely" side of me, which is not a large or developed as many of you might think, thought "awww... it will be so nice to have a group of partners that will walk this journey with me". The cynical side of me thought "oh great, here goes 3 hours every week that I won't get back".

Covenants are part of our Methodist heritage. John Wesley encouraged members of the early Methodist movement to meet regularly in Methodist Class Meetings. They would confess their sins to one another, pray together, and be healed together. This is where the early leaders of the Methodist movement were nurtured and equipped.

The Old and New Testaments are a collection of covenant stories. In these stories we learn of leaders within Israel who were nurtured and equipped by God for the call God was placing upon them.

The Abrahamic covenant promised land, descendants, and prosperity. Exodus 19.5 tells us that if the Israelites could "obey" God's voice, and keep God's covenant, then they would be God's "treasured possession out of all the peoples".

The Davidic covenant established David's house, throne, and kingdom.

And then there is the new covenant which was established a new relationship between God and humans, which was mediated by Jesus. This new covenant was different. This new covenant was not limited only to the nation of Israel. Jews and Gentiles would now be blessed and protected through the new covenant. From front to back the Bible is a covenant. And that is where our scripture reading brings us.

"Then what is the advantage has the Jew? What is the value of circumcision"

These questions are precisely what Paul wants to get to the bottom of. And for us reading the text today through our twenty-first century Christian lenses we assume the answer will be "none". Circumcision was not about getting in or staying in God's favor. Circumcision was meant to identify those who were already in. If circumcision was meant to separate Israel from the rest of the nations, a physical mark of their covenant with God, where does this fit into the new covenant established through Christ? Paul does not side-step his question about the advantage the Jews have over the Gentiles. In verse two he addresses the question head on.

Israel had been entrusted by God with the "oracles of God", aka the Scriptures. These oracles had been written down long ago, by the generations of Abraham, Moses, and David, for the use of future generations. And who comprises the future generations: Paul and the Gentile church.

N.T. Wright, puts it like this: "The covenant was there to put to rights, to deal with evil and restore God's justice and order the cosmos".

Since September 9th our confirmands have been in covenant with one another and with you, I bet most of you here did not know that we as a congregation entered into that covenant.

By joining our confirmation class they covenanted to attend and actively participate in worship, attend weekly lessons (missing no more than 3), and attend an end of the year retreat. That was their end of the covenant. And in exchange our teachers (Sarah Lynn, Haley, and Patty) along with our high school mentors agreed to teach them and share the oracles of God with them.

As a congregation we covenanted to help them by teaching them the faith. That's why Jay Steadman did not mind a group of loud 6th, 7th, and 8th graders interrupting a Sunday school lesson he was trying to teach. That's why when this group would approach you in between services and barraged you with hard questions about your own relationship with God you cheerfully answered them.

Israel had been entrusted by God, through covenants that guaranteed prosperity and protection, to share the oracles of God with future generations. What really had transpired in the gap between generations? Was Israel faithful? Israel was called to be a faithful servant of God, to obey God's laws, to be a light to the nations. That was the purpose of the Torah!

The Torah was intended to enable Israel with the ability to preserve the oracles of God and be a light to the nations. However, over time and generations the Torah took the place of the oracles. For some, it became more important or simply easier to fulfill the requirements of Torah law rather than keeping and preserving the oracles which had been entrusted to Israel. But Israel had been unfaithful, and Paul knew this better than anyone else.

Our confirmands can tell you why Paul would know this just as well, if not better than anyone else. Before he was the Apostle Paul, Paul was a Jewish Pharisee who painstakingly persecuted the early church. Through these persecutions Paul was in fact violating many of the oracles and laws he, as Jew, had been chosen to preserve. Israel had been charged by God to not only save these stories for future generations, but was also charged to be an example of how to live for future generations.

What Paul is saying here is that Israel had been unfaithful.

Paul does not mean that Israel had lost its faith in God or simply became a band of unbelievers. Israel had been unfaithful to God's commission.

Paul even goes so far as to use Israel's own stories to explain their unfaithfulness. Paul was not writing down new ideas, he was simply uses what David had written. Psalm 51, this is the same theme that is scattered through second Samuel chapters eleven and twelve. Paul quotes the Psalm and points to what vindication Israel could have rightly suffered as a sinful nation. No reader of this letter, who was familiar with the psalter would fail to miss the unquoted verses within the theme of Romans 3. There is no escaping God's righteousness. David knew that and so did the reader of this letter.

A covenant relationship only works if both parties enter into the agreement knowing they are in it for the long-haul. This is one of the premises of marriage. We do not marry our spouse and become partners with them because we know they are without flaw or are perfect. The covenant group I was forced into joined during my first week's at Wesley did not kick me out of the group if I did not meet the prescribed agreement among us. If a confirmand was unable to meet a requirement of our confirmation class, or began show signs of disinterest Sarah Lynn, Haley, and Patty would not kick them out of the class and banish them from the group.

These punishments might seem justified or appropriate to some but that is not the point of entering into a covenant relationship. When we read the stories of the Old and New Testament and see Israel's unfaithfulness to God's commission, it would be easy for us to assume that Israel would receive a just punishment. It would be easy for us to assume that God would judge Israel as nation, because the covenant was built upon a nation and not individuals, and condemn them for their unfaithfulness.

But you see, that's not how grace works. And what God does is open this covenant to all: Jews AND Gentiles. This new covenant, opened and available to all people, is about the way in which God addresses our unfaithfulness through the cross and the resurrection of Jesus. After all, this what what the covenant was intended to do in the first place. Our unfaithfulness, our rejection of the covenant does not separate us from God. My sins, your sins do not keep us away from God.

This is what Paul is getting at when he says that true circumcision is not "something external or physical".

In the last verse of chapter two, Paul says, "a person is a Jew who is one inwardly, and real circumcision is a matter of the heart - it is spiritual and NOT literal". This means that we can have all of the outward signs that we want of our faith.

It does not matter how many "Jesus fish" you have on the back of your minivan. You can wear a cross around our neck, show up to church every Sunday without fail, or even participate in a small group; but if we have not opened our hearts to be marked by the Holy Spirit then it's all for nothing.

Last weekend I had the chance to go on a retreat, to go camping with our confirmation class. We braved rustic cabins, spiders, no cell phone service, technology glitches and weird howls in the night to open ourselves up to be marked by God. We opened our hearts to the opportunity to have the Holy Spirit work through us.

We gathered to learn what it means to grow, give, serve, and share as a follower of Jesus. We learned that it is through growing, giving, serving and sharing that our hearts are circumcised by God.

On Sunday morning, just as we were getting ready to leave and head back home to he soccer and lacrosse games that were scheduled I told our confirmands that when our hearts are marked by the Holy Spirit that we cannot be separated from God, even through our unfaithfulness and sin. It is when our hearts are circumcised by our faith in Jesus Christ that we are made one with God. It's not an outward symbol. And it is what keeps us connected with God through our unfaithfulness.

Romans 3:21-26 - I Like Big Buts

Jason Micheli

Pentecost

*But now, apart from law, the righteousness of God has been disclosed, and is
attested by the law and the prophets, the righteousness of God through faith in
Jesus Christ for all who believe. For there is no distinction, since all have
sinned and fall short of the glory of God; they are now justified by his grace
as a gift, through the redemption that is in Christ Jesus, whom God put
forward as a sacrifice of atonement by his blood, effective through faith. He
did this to show his righteousness, because in his divine forbearance he had
passed over the sins previously committed; it was to prove at the present time
that he himself is righteous and that he justifies the one who has faith in Jesus.*

- Romans 3:21-26

After a recent cataclysmic national event that I won't specify, I was
speaking on the phone with my mother who, like many of you, had
fallen into a despondent, black malaise.

"Maybe I will move to Canada" she said and sighed.

"Canada! They eat ketchup flavored Doritos in Canada—how is
that a thing?! And Canada is responsible for Celine Dion and
Nickelback. Think about that, Mom: Justin Bieber and Tom Ford don't
even crack the Top Ten of Canadiens for whom Canada should have to
issue a global apology. Though Canada did give the world that babe
who played Kim in *24*."

"She's beautiful."

"Yes, she is…" I said and immediately my mind wandered to
the film in which Kim costarred with Raylan Givens, *The Girl Next
Door*.

"Jason? Jason, are you still there?"

"Huh? Yeah, I'm still here. I was just…thinking. Look, forget
this Canada nonsense. Mom, you hate the snow and no matter how
much I begged you as a kid you never let me grow a mullet."

"I hate mullets."

"See, forget Canada. I'll tell you, though, if I just had a Jew in my family tree I'd move to Israel, at their least president is actually a conservative."

"But my grandparents were Jewish."

"But *what*?!"

"My grandparents...they were both Jewish. "

"But...but...but...that means my great-grandparents were *Jewish*."

"Uh, huh" my mother said blankly, clearly not registering that this was a seismic revelation for someone like me who, let's just say, is salaried and pensioned NOT to be Jewish.

"But...but...but...*that means I'm Jewish*" I whispered while turning down the volume on my iPhone.

"Yeah, I guess it does."

No joke, my next thoughts, in rapid-fire succession:

1. Holy bleep, how have I not heard about this before?!

2. No wonder I'm so funny.

3. Thank God I'm already circumcised.

4. I could spin this into a book! Christian clergyman discovers his previously unknown Jewish identity. It practically writes itself.

As for the screen, it'd be the perfect follow up to *La La Land* for Ryan Gosling.

As soon as I got off the phone with my mom I pitched the book idea to my editor. I'd even come up with some snappy titles such as: *Riddler on the Roots*, *Goy Meets God*, and, my personal favorite, *Trans-Gentile*.

Nevertheless, my editor replied that until I actually convert and move myself and my family to the Promised Land, what I had was a good idea for a sermon.

Not a book.

Of course, that same editor came up with a terrible book title like *Cancer Is Funny* so I figured what the hell does he know? Besides, I've always acted as though I'm God's gift to the world and now, as it turns out, I really am—I'm chosen!

I've got to find out more about what that means! I thought.

In the weeks and months that followed, I studied up.

I researched the State of Israel's Right of Return rules. I qualify.

I tested my DNA through ancestry.com, the results of which bore out what my mother had told me, that I am of Jewish lineage by way of Austria.

And thanks to Ghengis Khan raping and pillaging his way across Europe I also have some Mongolian in me too, and, according to the customer service person at ancestry.com, chances are, you have some Mongolian in you too.

DNA in hand, I consulted with Rabbi Hayim Herring about what books he recommends to potential converts. At his advice I read the *Tanakh*, *Living a Jewish Life* by Anita Diamant, *Judaism's Ten Best Ideas* by Arthur Green, and *To Life: A Celebration of Jewish Being and Thinking* by Harold Kushner.

And, because Rabbi Herring explained to me that Judaism is a religion that developed out of its celebrations, I read *The Jewish Way* by Irving Greenberg, a book about the Jewish holy days.

Including the holy day of Pentecost.

Or, as my people say, Shavu'ot.

———

Shavu'ot—the Festival of Weeks, five weeks, Penta-cost, after Passover.

Shavu'ot—the Jewish holiday that brings Peter and the disciples and a crowd of thousands of pilgrims to Jerusalem to celebrate.

They're not there waiting for the Holy Spirit. They're gathered to celebrate Pentecost, the holy day when they remember God giving to them, on Mt. Sinai, the Torah, the Law.

If Shavu'ot is the day when the Spirit descends upon the disciples, then Shavu'ot is the day by which we should interpret the descent of the Holy Spirit upon the disciples.

As a Gentile, I've always preached Pentecost straight up and simply as the arrival of the Holy Spirit, or, to be more exact, as the arrival of a previously not present Holy Spirit—as though, ascending in to heaven, the Risen Christ, like Jon Cena, tags in and the Holy Spirit takes over.

But with my new Jewish eyes, I see that that can't be because the Spirit is everywhere all over the Old Testament, the Hebrew Bible, doing and moving.

Not to mention, Luke—the author of Acts—has already told us that the Holy Spirit overshadowed Mary, compelled Jesus's first sermon in Nazareth, and baptized Jesus into his baptism of vicarious repentance.

So if the arrival of the Holy Spirit is not the point of this Pentecost passage in Acts 2, then what is?

———

When the Holy Spirit descends upon the Pentecost pilgrims, the crowd becomes bewildered.

But Peter, Luke says, stands up and proclaims the Gospel to them. And that phrasing, that odd way of beginning a sentence "But Peter..." is Luke's clue for you that Peter is not deciding on his own to stand up and preach, that an unseen agency is working upon him, that he is being compelled by God, by the Holy Spirit, to proclaim what God has done in Jesus Christ.

And at the end of his preaching, Luke tells us, Peter's listeners are cut to the heart—note the passive. They're acted upon.

An unseen agency is working upon them too, compelling them to believe.

Then Luke concludes by telling us that on that Pentecost 3,000 were added to the People of God.

Maybe you Gentiles don't know this—in the Bible numbers are always important. Numbers are always the clue to unlocking the story's meaning.

It's not incidental that Luke ends his story of this Shavu'ot with the number 3,000 being added to God's People because on the first Shavu'ot 3,000 were subtracted from God's People.

On the first Shavu'ot, while Moses is on top of Mt. Sinai receiving the Law from God, the Torah—which begins "Thou shalt have no other gods before me"—the Israelites were busy down below making God into an idol—which is but a form of making God into our own image.

When Moses comes down from Mt. Sinai, he sees them worshiping a golden calf, and Moses responds by ordering the Levites to draw their swords and kill 3,000 of the idolaters.

So when Luke tells you that 3,000 were added to God's People on that Pentecost day he wants you to remember the 3,000 subtracted from God's People that other Pentecost day.

Where 3,000 committed idolatry, 3,000 now believe.

Those in the crowd, listening to Peter, they're no different than the crowd at the foot of Mt. Sinai.

They're every bit as susceptible to worship any god but God, every bit as prone to unbelief and unfaithfulness. They crucified God just over a month ago.

They're no different than the crowd at the foot of Mt. Sinai that first Shavu'ot.

What Luke wants you to see in this Pentecost story is the undoing of that Pentecost story, and he wants you to see that it's God's doing, not our own—God's faithfulness to us despite our unfaithfulness, God graciously overcoming our unbelief, our proclivity to idolatry and sin.

Luke wants you to see that this new 3,000 is the Living God's doing. The Holy Spirit's doing. The Spirit of the Crucified and Risen Christ's doing, compelling Peter—who before could never get his foot out of his mouth—to proclaim.

It's God's doing, calling out of, creating in, Peter's hearers, out of nothing, *faith*.

———

Luke shows us in the beginning of Acts what the Apostle Paul tells us in Romans.

After announcing his thesis—the good news—at the beginning of his letter to the Romans, Paul braces us with the bad news.

For the rest of chapter 1, all of chapter 2, and the beginning of chapter 3 Paul bears down with white-knuckles and surveys the extent of our captivity, our bondage to Sin.

He says our every sin starts with the same sin as at Mt. Sinai on that first Shavu'ot: our failure to worship God, giving up God for other gods.

Our first sin also begets our wickedness and our malice. It gives rise to our greed and our lust and our violence. It spawns our slander and our deceit, our hypocrisy and our infidelity, even our gossip and our haughtiness and our hardness of heart.

Over almost 3 chapters, Paul unrolls the rap sheet of our sin until not one of us left un-indicted.

All have sinned, Paul says, religious and unreligious alike.

No one is righteous, Paul laments, not a single one of us.

No one seeks God. No one desires peace.

Our mouths are quick to curse, our hands are quick to stuff our own pockets, our feet are too quick to shed blood, Paul says.

None of us is any different than those 3,000 at the foot of Mt. Sinai on the first *Shavu'ot* worshipping anything other than God.

There is no distinction between any of us—we're all ungodly.

Paul's relentless litany of our sinfulness goes on and on for almost three chapters, an overwhelming avalanche of awful truth-telling and indictments.

For almost three chapters, Paul keeps raising the stakes, tightening the screws, shining the light hotter and brighter on our crimes, implicating each and every one of us.

Until, what you expect next from Paul is the word "if."

———

If.

If you turn away from sin...

If you turn towards God...

If you repent...

If you...plead for God's mercy...

If you seek God's forgiveness...

If you believe...

If you put your faith in him...

If...

Then...

God will justify you.

Paul relentlessly unrolls the rap sheet until every last one of our names is indicted. Not one of us is righteous and every one of us is deserving of God's wrath, Paul says.

This sounds like an altar call coming, right? And the word you expect Paul to use next is "if."

If you repent and believe.

Instead of *if* **but**:

"But now" Paul says.

"But now, apart from the Law (apart from Religion) the rectifying power of God has been revealed...the rectification by God through the faithfulness of Jesus Christ.."

There couldn't be a bigger but.

Martin Luther says that "but now" is a fish-hook shaped word that catches us all.

There couldn't be a bigger but. It's the hinge on which the Gospel turns:

We're all unrighteous.

We're all entangled in Sin.

But now—God.

The rectifying power of God has invaded our world without a single "if."

The rectifying power of God—the power of God to make us right and to put our world to rights—has invaded in the faithfulness of Jesus Christ upon the Cross.

The grace of God has invaded unilaterally—without prior condition or presupposition.

Without a single "if."

There is nothing you need to do for it to be true for you.

Our justification is not God's response to us; it's God's gracious initiative for us.

As far as God is concerned, true love doesn't wait.

If you repent, then I'll...

If you seek forgiveness, then I'll...

If you believe, then I'll...

If you have faith in me, then I'll...

No.

No ifs. No conditions.

"But now..." Paul announces.

God's love doesn't wait for us. To rescue us.

All have sinned.

All fall short of God's glory.

But now-

All are being rectified by the uncontingent grace of God in Jesus Christ.

There are no "ifs," just this big but: "But now..." God has done this. It's gift. Sheer un-contingent, irrevocable gift.

It's just like the song says.

You once were lost BUT NOW you've been found—note the passive again.

You didn't find. You've been found not because you went searching for God, but because in Jesus Christ has sought you out and bought you with his blood.

————

During Lent I gave up bacon. Just to see, you know, in case the UMC ever folds, if I could hack it as a Hebrew (I made it 3 days).

During Lent I also read the *The Jewish Way* where I learned that if I ever did convert to Judaism, then I'd need to choose a Hebrew name.

"What's the name of that talking donkey in the Old Testament?" my wife asked pointedly.

The Jewish Way by Irving Greenberg also reminded me what I'd forgotten since seminary: that the covenant (*berit* as my people say) God makes with Moses on Mt. Sinai on that first Pentecost, the promise God makes to Moses on Mt. Sinai, is conditional.

"You will be my treasured People" God promises "**but** you must keep all my commandments."

It's conditional.

"You will be my People, **but** you must be faithful to my commands."

It's conditional.

"I will be your God, **but** you must remain faithful and obey."

It's contingent.

"**If** you keep faith in me, **then** I will be your God and you will be my People."

It's not just on Mt. Sinai. So much of our lives and our relationships are littered with ifs.   If you make it up to me, then I'll take you back.

If you promise not to spend it on drugs, then I'll give you a handout.

If I'm just a better wife, then he'll love me/then he'll stop drinking/then he won't abuse me anymore.

If I just get better grades, get into that college, get that job, then they'll be proud of me/then maybe Dad will finally tell me that he loves me.

If/then conditionality is hard-wired into us.

I forgive you, **but** I won't forget.

Paul would say that's how captives speak.

We do it with God too.

We take this big but at the beginning of Paul's Gospel sentence and we put it at the end of our sentences.

You are justified by grace as a gift through the redemption that is in Jesus   Christ, **but** first you must believe, we say.

We move Paul's big but to the end of our sentences.

God in Jesus Christ has given his life for you, crucified for you, **but** first you must repent.

The balance sheet of your life has been set right—not by anything you've done, by God's grace, **but** you must serve the poor, pray, go to church, give to the church.

We take this big but at the beginning of Paul's Gospel sentence and we put it at the end of our sentences. We turn it around and make it conditional: *If you have faith **then** you will be justified.*

Not only is that conditionality not Paul's Gospel, it contradicts what Luke shows us at Pentecost and what Paul tells us here in Romans.

The whole point of Paul's big "But now" is that by yourself, on your own, by your own power, you don't have the capacity to fulfill any of those conditions.

Your faith, your belief, your repentance, your service—none of it is a prerequisite for God's grace because all of it is a product of God's gracious doing.

"But now," Paul says, God has acted for us "apart from the Law," apart from any of our religious doing.

Just like the Holy Spirit at Pentecost undoing the unbelief of the first Pentecost, God acts for us in the faithfulness of Jesus Christ and his faith, Paul says, has the power to elicit our faith.

Jesus' faith isn't just prior; it's causative.

As Paul says in another letter, no one can say that Jesus is Lord except by his Holy Spirit.

As Paul puts it in this letter, in the next chapter, God calls into existence the things that do not exist—meaning, our faith.

Luke says that nothing is impossible for God, but the whole point of Paul's big "But" is that faith is impossible for us without God.

Your faith is not the exercise of your free will.

Your faith is a sign that God has freed your will from the Power of Sin.

Which means-

Whatever measure of faith you have, whether your faith is as tiny as a mustard seed or as massive as a mountain, it's the Holy Spirit's doing not your own.

It makes you proof of the God who invades our world without a single "if."

Such that now—now as a person of faith, as a person in whom the unconditional grace of God has created faith, there is nothing you *must* do.

You don't *have* to do anything.

The balance sheet of your life has been set right not by anything you've done, by what God has done.

You have been justified by the grace of God in Jesus Christ.

There's not a **but** at the end of that sentence. There is nothing now you *must* do.

Rather, as a person in whom the unconditional love of God has created faith, there is now so much you are **set free** to do.

———

Take it from a mensch like me, Paul's big "But" here in Romans 3, I think it just might be the most important word of the Gospel.

I do know the absence of any 'if' here is the Gospel.

Romans 3:9-20 - Junk in the Trunk

Jason Micheli

What then? Are we any better off? No, not at all; for we have already charged that all, both Jews and Greeks, are under the power of sin, as it is written: "There is no one who is righteous, not even one; there is no one who has understanding, there is no one who seeks God. All have turned aside, together they have become worthless; there is no one who shows kindness, there is not even one." "Their throats are opened graves; they use their tongues to deceive." "The venom of vipers is under their lips." "Their mouths are full of cursing and bitterness." "Their feet are swift to shed blood; ruin and misery are in their paths, and the way of peace they have not known." "There is no fear of God before their eyes."

Now we know that whatever the law says, it speaks to those who are under the law, so that every mouth may be silenced, and the whole world may be held accountable to God. For "no human being will be justified in his sight" by deeds prescribed by the law, for through the law comes the knowledge of sin.

- Romans 3:9-20

As many of you know, I do a lot of my work at Starbucks.

I have my reasons.

For one thing, I get more accomplished without Dennis pestering me to show him how his computer works.

But to be honest, the main reason I go to Starbucks is because I like to eavesdrop.

It's true. What ice cream and cheesecake were to the Golden Girls, eavesdropping is to me.

At Starbucks, I'm like a fly on the wall with a moleskin notebook under his wing.

I've been dropping eaves at coffee shops for as long as I've been a pastor and, until this week at least, I've never been caught.

This week I sat down at a little round table and started to sketch out a funeral sermon.

At the table to my left was a 20-something guy with ear phones in and an iPad out and a man-purse slung across his shoulder.

At the table to my right were two middle-aged women. They had a Bible and a couple of Beth Moore books on the table between them. And a copy of the *Mt Vernon Gazette*.

The first thing I noticed, though, was their perfume. It was so strong I could taste it in my coffee.

Now, in my defense I don't think I could properly be accused of eavesdropping considering just how loud the two women were talking. Like they wanted to be heard.

Their "Bible study" or whatever it had been was apparently over because the woman by the window closed the Bible and then commented out loud: "I really do need to get a new Bible. This one's worn out completely. I've just read it so much."

Not to be outdone, the woman across from her, parried, saying just as loudly: "I don't know what I'd do if I didn't spend time in the Word every day. I don't know what people do without the Lord."

'they do whatever they want" her friend by the window said.

And I said to myself, "Geez, I've sat next to two Flannery O"Connor characters."

I assumed that since they were actually reading the bible there was no way they attended this church, but just to make sure I gave them a double-take.

They had perfectly permed hair flecked with frosted highlights. And they had nails in which I could see the reflection of their large, costume jewelry.

"Baptists" I thought to myself.

They continued chatting over their lattes as the woman by the window flipped through the *Mt Vernon Gazette*. She stopped at a page and shook her head in disapproval.

Whether she actually said 'tsk, tsk, tsk," or I imagined it, I can't be sure.

The other woman looked down at the paper and said: "Oh, I heard about that. He was only 31."

"Did you hear it was an overdose?" the woman by the window said like a kid on Christmas morning.

And that's when I knew who they were gossiping about. I knew because I was sitting next to them writing that young man's funeral sermon.

"Did he know the Lord?" the woman asked.

"Probably not considering the lifestyle," the woman by the window said without pause.

They went on gossiping from there.

They used words like 'shameful."

They did not, I noticed, use words like 'sad" or 'tragic" or "unfortunate."

It wasn't long before the circumference of their conversation spun its way to encompass things like 'society and what's wrong with it," how parents need to pray their kids into the straight and narrow, and how 'this is what happens when our culture turns its back on God."

After a while they came to a lull in their conversation and the woman opposite the window, the one with the gaudy bedazzled cross on her neck, gazed down at the *Mt Vernon Gazette* and wondered out loud: "What do you say at a funeral like that?"

And without even looking at them, and with a volume that surprised me, I said: 'the same damn thing that"ll be said at your funeral."

They didn't even blush. But they did look at me awkwardly.

"I hardly think so," the woman by the window said, sizing me up and not looking very impressed with the sum of what she saw.

And so I laid my cards down: "Well, I probably won't be preaching your funeral, but I will be preaching his."

And then I pointed at her theatrically worn Bible, the one resting on top of her copy of *A Heart Like His* by Beth Moore, and I said: "If you actually took that seriously you'd shut up right now."

———

"No one is righteous, not one."

Sounds a little harsh, right? I mean, no one?

Just try filling in the blank of Paul's assertion. Think of the best person you can and stick them down inside Paul's sentence and listen to how it sounds.

No one is righteous, not one, not even Mother Theresa.

No one is righteous, not one, not even Gandhi.

No one is righteous, not one, not even your Mother (Happy Mother's Day).

When you hear today's scripture text the first time through, it sounds like this is Exhibit A for everything people hate about Christianity.

Here's this God who made us and then made a measuring stick that was just a little bit higher than the best of us and a lot higher than most of us.

But to hear it that way is to miss who Paul is speaking to and where this falls in Paul's letter.

In case you're just tuning in, so far Paul has spent chapters 1 and 2 of his letter pointing out everything that's wrong with the world. Everything that's broken in God's creation.

And in chapters 1 and 2, Paul makes his case by pointing his finger at "those people."

"Them."

Not the good, every-Sunday people at church in Rome, but those other people—"society." You know, those people? The "lost" people who don't believe in God, who don't attend worship, don't raise their children right.

Those people.

They're greedy, Paul says. Violent even. They've got no morals or values.

"Just listen to the way they talk" says Paul, "all cursing and slander."

Those people.

They've broken the institution of marriage and the family. They just hop from one bed to the next, one mate to another, like people are just a means to an end.

Those people.

They've got no commitment. No decency.

Paul spends chapters 1 and 2 pointing at 'those people" and ticking off their every sin and flaw.

And with each and every indictment, you can imagine, as the accusations build, the members at First Church Rome nodded right along with self-satisfied smiles on their faces.

You can imagine them saying to themselves: 'that's right, that's exactly how those people are. Thank God I'm not like those people."

And that's Paul's rhetorical trap because in chapter 3 he turns his aim at the good People of God, and he says: "No one is righteous, not one."

Which is Paul's way of saying: not even you.

And then Paul hits them—us—with this battering ram of accusations about how we sin every day with our minds and our lips and our hands and feet, by what we do and by what we leave undone.

And Paul lifts those accusations, one by one, word for word, straight out of scripture.

And *that's* Paul's point.

That's Paul's point when he says we're not justified by the law, by scripture.

————

You see, the takeaway from today's text isn't that you're a perpetual disappointment to God. If that's what you leave with then you've missed what Paul's doing here.

The takeaway is that belonging to a religious community doesn't make you any closer to God than anyone else. Believing in the bible doesn't make you a better person than anyone else because that same bible indicts you too.

You may go to church every Sunday but the Book of Micah says God hates your praise if there's a single poor person in the streets.

You may be a good mother and love your kids, but the Book of Mark says if you don't love Jesus more, then...

You may be a clergy person like me, you might've given your whole career to God, but the best the Book of Matthew has to say about that is that I'm like a white-washed tomb, a hypocrite with lies on the inside.

Don't confuse your place in the pews with a place in God's favor—that's Paul's point—because the only advantage this (the bible) gives us is that it tells the truth about us.

Who we really are.

"No one is righteous. Not one."

————

The woman by the window actually did shut up for a moment, clearly trying to figure out how this had become a three-person conversation.

And then it hit her: "Have you been eavesdropping on us?"

"Of course not," I lied.

"Why don't you mind your own business?" she scolded.

"But that's just it," I said, "it is my business. I'm a preacher and so I couldn't help but notice that I had two Pharisees sitting next to me."

She narrowed her eyes and lowered her voice: "Listen, young man. I've been saved. I love the Lord, talk to him and read his Word every day."

"Apparently you've not retained very much" I mumbled.

"What's that supposed to mean?" she asked with mustered outrage.

"It means you're no better than that guy over there" and I pointed to a homeless guy who was nursing his coffee and muttering to himself.

"In fact, you're not good at all. And neither am I. None of us is in a position to judge anyone else, and someone with a worn-out bible should already know that."

I thought that I'd just played a trump card. The end.

"Well, isn't that exactly what you're doing right now? she asked me. And suddenly I felt the tables turning.

"Uh, what do you mean?" I asked.

"Well, it sounds like you've been eavesdropping on us for the last 10 minutes and judging us the whole time."

I felt myself blush: "Not the *whole* time."

"I bet you started judging us before you even heard what we were talking about."

"I did not" I lied. "Don't forget you're talking to a pastor."

And I thought that was the end of it, but then she turned her chairs towards me, like we were all together, and she asked:

"So, what makes *you* do it? Why are you so quick to stick your nose in other people's junk and judge them?"

I considered punting on her question, telling her I had work to do and leaving it at that.

But she'd caught me eavesdropping so I thought I should balance out my vice with a little virtue.

I told her the truth: "Probably because I have junk of my own that I don't know what to do with."

"Me too" she said, and suddenly she dropped her guard like we were fellow addicts at an AA Meeting.
She said: "I'm constantly carrying around things I'm not proud of, things I'm ashamed of, things I try to keep locked and hidden away, because I don't know what to do with them."

And then her friend, the one opposite the window, sipped her coffee and then said: "Me three."

I've been a pastor long enough to know that if you'd been sitting there you too would've said...

"Me four."

Because it's true of all of us.

We condemn and we criticize and we label and we gossip and we judge.

We raise an eyebrow at other people's mistakes, other people's sins, other people's problems—because we're carrying around our own junk and we don't know what to do with it.

———

Paul shows us what to do with our junk.

Paul shows us what to do with the worst secrets about ourselves that we carry around with us.

You can't forget that when Paul directs his attack in chapter 3 at religious people, the first person Paul has in mind is Paul.

You can't forget that when Paul levels the accusation that "No one is righteous, not one" Paul's speaking in the *first person* before he's speaking about any other person.

Paul cursed and condemned Christians. Paul encouraged executions and stood by smiling while Christians were stoned to death.

Paul's the one whose throat was an open grave.

Paul's the one who used his tongue to deceive and had venom on his lips.

Paul's the one whose mouth was full of bitterness, whose feet were swift to shed blood.

Paul's the one who knew not the way of peace...until he met the Resurrected Christ.

And after he meets the Risen Christ, Paul is free to own up to all of it.

All the junk he would otherwise want to hide and deny and push down and repress and keep locked and hidden away.

Paul shows us what we can do with our junk.

Paul shows us that if we're more convinced of God's grace than the sin we're convinced we must keep secret from everyone, then we can open up this junk we carry around with us and we can say:

"No one is righteous, no one, especially not me.

Look at what I've done.

This is who I was.

These are the words I spoke in anger that can never be taken back

This is the relationship I pretended was fine until it unraveled away.

These are the kids I took for granted until they were grown and gone.

This is the person I see in the mirror every day and have never learned to love.

This is the addiction I always insisted didn't have the better of me.

This is the insecurity that masks itself as cynicism.

These are all the people I refused to forgive.

This is the person closest to me I cheated on...

But God...God forgives...all of it."

Paul shows us that our worst junk can become a living, breathing example of what God's amazing grace can do.

Which is kind of a shame.

Because I've been a pastor long enough to know that most of you pretend you're not so desperate as to need a grace that's anywhere near amazing.

Most of you pretend you're not actually carting this junk around and have no idea what to do with it.

For many of you, church is the last place where you're really *you*, and Sunday morning is the time of the week you're the least open about who you really are.

Church is where you grin and pretend like it's all good and you've got your **** together.

Many of you have come to church for years so determined to not let anyone find out what's in here (junk in the trunk) that you've never trusted Jesus Christ in here (your heart).

And that's a shame.

Because Paul shows us — the things we're most burdened by are the things the world most needs to hear.

Paul shows us that if we open this up and admit that no one is righteous, not even me. . . and here I'll give you a "for instance"

Paul shows us that if we can say that then what someone else can hear is: "If God's grace is for them . . . then it's even for me . . ."

———

Yesterday afternoon nearly 500 gathered to celebrate that young man's funeral.

We sang "Amazing Grace."

We heard a reading from Paul's Letter to the Philippians. It was different words but the same meaning. And I preached the Gospel.

The same message I'd preach at any of your deaths.

After the funeral, I was walking past the receiving line, which started here at the altar and snaked its way to the other end of the building, and one of the deceased's friends grabbed my elbow and said to me: "If what you said is true for him, then it's true for me too . . . right?"

And I said: "Yeah."

And he let go of my elbow and said, 'thanks for sharing that."

Romans 4:1-5, 13-7 - Open Hearts. Open Minds. Open Doors.

Taylor Mertins

What then are we to say was gained by Abraham, our ancestor according to the flesh? For if Abraham was justified by works, he has something to boast about, but not before God. For what does the scripture say? "Abraham believed God, and it was reckoned to him as righteousness." Now to one who works, wages are not reckoned as a gift but as something due. But to one who without works trusts him who justifies the ungodly, such faith is reckoned as righteousness. For the promise that he would inherit the world did not come to Abraham or to his descendants through the law but through the righteousness of faith. If it is the adherents of the law who are to be the heirs, faith is null and the promise is void. For the law brings wrath; but where there is no law, neither is there violation. For this reason it depends on faith, in order that the promise may rest on grace and be guaranteed to all his descendants, not only to the adherents of the law but also to those who share the faith of Abraham (for he is the father of all of us, as it is written, "I have made you the father of many nations") -- in the presence of the God in whom he believed, who gives life to the dead and calls into existence the things that do not exist. Abraham believed God, and it was reckoned to him as righteousness.

- Romans 4.1-5, 13-17

There are many many many versions of Christianity. And not just denominations like Presbyterians, Episcopalians, and Baptists; even within something like the United Methodist Church there is a great myriad of ideas about what it means to be the church. For instance: There are 7 UMCs in Staunton, and we could all use the same text on Sunday morning, and just about everything else would be completely different from one another.

But the one thing that might unite all churches, almost more than baptism or communion, is a desire to appear as welcoming and inclusive as possible.

All you need to do is check a church website, or bulletin, or marquee and you can find a self-made description that says something

45

like: we are an open, friendly, inclusive, and welcoming church. Or just try asking someone about their church and you're likely to hear: "we love everybody!"

In the United Methodist Church, we like to say we have open hearts, open minds, and open doors.

What a righteous slogan.

Inclusivity, being open, they're quite the buzzwords these days. Rather than appearing at all judgmental, we want people to know that we accept all people. Rather than seeming prejudiced, we want everyone to know that they are welcome. Rather than looking at people based on their outward appearance, we want to the world to know that we care about the content of one's character.

But the truth is, there are a great number of people who have been ignored, if not rejected, by congregations claiming to be inclusive (including our own).

A couple weeks ago I preached a sermon on the mission of the church. I made the claim that instead of being consumed by a desire to fill the pews, instead of trying to make the world a better place, the church is called to be the better place that God has already made in the world. And as the better place, church should be the one place where no one is ever lonely. I must've said that last part no less than three times from the pulpit.

And when we finished worship, most of us walked up the stairs to the Social Hall for a time of food and fellowship. Like we usually do, a long line was formed and one by one we filled our plates and sat down.

The time difference between proclaiming the sermon and sitting down to eat could not have been more than 30 minutes. And yet there was a young family who were here with us in worship for the very first time, who sat alone in our social hall the entire time. And there was an older gentleman, who has served the needs of this church longer than I've been alive, who sat by himself for nearly the entire time.

It is not possible for any church, even St. John's, to be "inclusive" of everyone. And not necessarily for the reasons we might think. We might not judge others for the stereotypical ways often publicized about the church like being homophobic, or racist, or elitist (though there is plenty of that). No, we also reject others for mental illness, politically different or incorrect views, or for poor social skills and status.

We reject people for all sorts of reasons.

Years ago, when I first entered seminary, I went on a bike ride with some friends to another house full of seminarians. We represented the great mosaic of mainline protestant Christianity and we quickly began addressing why each of us was attracted to the particular church we would serve in the future. The Episcopalian talked about her love of the Book of Common Prayer and being united with Christians all over the world who say the exact same words whenever they get together. The Baptist talked about the beauty of believer's baptism and getting to bring adults into God's flock.

One of the Methodists, me, talked about the wonder of God's prevenient grace, a love that is offered to all without cost or judgment. But then I went on to express my chief disappointment: Our slogan of open hearts, open minds, open doors. I joked about how many Methodist churches regularly lock their doors, how many of them are filled with people whose minds are already made up about God and others, and how many of them have people with hearts that have no desire to be open to the strange new reality of God's kingdom.

To be honest, I got pretty fired up about it. After all, it was the beginning of seminary and I was trying to show off.

But I meant what I said. Our slogan is something we can strive for, but it is not a fair description of who we are. There will always be a newcomer who sits in a pew by herself without anyone coming over to say hello. There will always be a family that risks being ostracized by coming to church only to being judged from afar. There will always be sermon series that make people feel like they are not welcome into the fold of God's grace.

So I went on and on about this until I looked at the other Methodist whose face had turned bright red. "Is everything okay?" I asked. He paused and then said, "My Dad was on the committee at General Conference that created our slogan. I think it's the *best* thing about the United Methodist Church."

We have a slogan, a nice and pretty slogan that we should strive for, but oftentimes we fall short. When we fall short, we do so because of sin. Sin captivates us in a way that makes it virtually impossible for

47

any church to "unconditionally accept" everyone who comes through the door.

We judge others based on physical and outward appearance. We make assumptions about families for a myriad of reasons. We shake our heads in disgust about couples that do not fit the normative mold that society has established.

And we should be cautious about advertising or describing ourselves as such. We might think we're righteous enough to live by the slogan, we can even hope for it, but we are far from it.

Only Jesus, the one in whom we live and move, is capable of a truly open heart, open mind, open door ministry because Jesus was God in the flesh. Jesus was righteous.

But what about Abraham? Paul uses this part of his letter to the Romans to use Abraham as an example of righteousness. Abraham was the one who was called to leave the land of his ancestors and family to go where God called him. Abraham was the one in whom the covenant between God and God's people was made. Abraham was the one who was promised to become the father of many nations. Abraham was the one who believed God and it was reckoned to him as righteousness.

Should we follow Abraham's example? Would that make us more inclusive and righteous? Could we keep our slogan of open hearts, open minds, open doors?

Here's the thing: Abraham did nothing to earn this honor and distinction from God. As Paul puts it, Abraham has no ground for boasting.

Whenever we read about the story of Abraham, whether in worship or in a bible study, he is often lauded for his journey into the unknown, for his faith and steadfast commitment to the Lord, and for his perseverance through suffering and tribulation. But his relationship with God, his faith being reckoned as righteousness, is only possible because of God's faith in him. Abraham is righteous because God called him and empowered him to go into a strange new world.

Abraham, rather than being the perfect model for inclusivity and righteousness and faithfulness, is an example of a justified sinner. Abraham is one of many unlikely individuals whom God reshapes for God's purposes. Abraham is chosen not because of anything he has done, but because of God who can do anything.

God is the one who worked in and through Abraham's life, and not the other way around. Abraham does not justify himself, or transform himself, or redeem himself. That's what God does.

And the same holds true for us today.

We can have the perfect advertising campaign, with our slogan in big capital letters, but that does not redeem our sinful actions and behaviors. We might think we are righteous and that we are "color-blind" or "LGBTQ affirming" or "economically transparent" but we are nevertheless sinners in need of God's grace and forgiveness. We can even leave the church doors unlocked all week long, but we will still be broken and in need of God's redeeming love.

This passage, this beautiful piece of theology from Romans, is about more than the example of Abraham and why we need to have faith. Paul's emphasis is on the fact that God made Abraham righteous. That God has freely poured out grace on the ungodly, people like us. And that God's gift of Jesus Christ to us and to the world is grossly unmerited and undeserved, and yet it is given to us.

She came to church pretty regularly but she kept to herself. She'd sit off at the end of a pew and keep her head down so as not to attract too much attention. Whenever it was time to sing, she would stand up with everyone else but her voice never made it higher than a whisper. When it came time to say the Lord's Prayer she would properly bow her head and mouth the words. But whenever the congregation was invited to the front to receive communion, she never left her seat.

Most of the church was preoccupied with thoughts about their own sins or about where they would eat lunch after the service to notice the woman who remained in her pew while they were feasting on the body and the blood. But the pastor noticed.

After a couple months he caught her after church, and wanted to know why she participated in almost every part of worship, but not in communion. She said, "I don't feel like I deserve it."

That, my friends, is the whole point. We don't deserve it. You don't, and I don't. None of us have earned God's salvation, there's no list of things we can check off in order to get into heaven. This bread and this cup, the cross and the empty tomb, they are unmerited and undeserved gifts from God to us.

We cannot have a church that is open hearts, open minds, and open doors because we are already in it. Our presence, our sinfulness, makes it impossible to be a totally inclusive community.

Only Christ, only God, only the Spirit have open hearts, open minds, open doors. Only the triune God opens up the floodgates of grace to wash away our sins. Only the triune God opens up our eyes to view others without judgment or wrath or fear or anger. Only the triune God opens the doors of the church, the faithful community, to feast at the table that gives us a foretaste of heaven on earth.

Only the triune God gives life to the dead and calls into existence the things that do not exist. To God be the glory. Amen.

Romans 5:1-11 - The Wedding Jacket

Teer Hardy

Therefore, since we are justified by faith, we have peace with God through our Lord Jesus Christ, through whom we have obtained access to this grace in which we stand; and we boast in our hope of sharing the glory of God. And not only that, but we also boast in our sufferings, knowing that suffering produces endurance, and endurance produces character, and character produces hope, and hope does not disappoint us, because God's love has been poured into our hearts through the Holy Spirit that has been given to us. For while we were still weak, at the right time Christ died for the ungodly. Indeed, rarely will anyone die for a righteous person – though perhaps for a good person someone might actually dare to die. But God proves his love for us in that while we still were sinners Christ died for us. Much more surely then, now that we have been justified by his blood, will we be saved through him from the wrath of God. For if while we were reconciled to God through the death of his Son, much more surely, having been reconciled, will we be saved by his life. But more than that, we even boast in God through our Lord Jesus Christ, through whom we have now received reconciliation. For while we were still weak, at the right time Christ died for the ungodly.

- Romans 5.1-11

This past week the Miami Heat & San Antonio Spurs wrapped up the NBA season. Whether you are a Heat fan, a Spurs fan, or could care less about the NBA because college basketball is 100 times better and the game played in the NBA allows player basically run up and down the court without dribbling the ball, it was hard to hide from the 24/7 coverage ESPN and the other sports media outlets provided us with. One story in particular stood out from the rest.

On Tuesday night the Heat and Spurs battled in what some have described as one of the all time greatest NBA playoff games of all time, some would not agree with that statement because the NBA is more about entertaining fans and presenting entertainment rather than upholding the game of basketball, but others are saying that it was infact one of the greatest NBA games ever played. With less than a minute left in regulation the Heat were down 5 points and many fans began to stream out of the American Airlines arena, disappointed that LeBron James and his teammates had been unable to play the game of basketball at a NBA championship caliber level for 4 quarters in a row. Little did these fair-weather fans know, that the Heat would tie up the game with less than a minute to go, send game six into overtime and win by a 3 point margin, 103-100. The fans that left the game early, those folks who did not want to stick around for the final few seconds of the game were not allowed to re-enter the arena.

They were not invested in the team and were, as some sports commentators have argued, "fair-weather fans". Those fans that left early had done little more than put on the appearance of being a Miami Heat fan and showed up to the American Airlines area. That was it. They claimed the name of the Miami Heat, a team that until LeBron James and Chris Bosh joined the roster had been at the bottom of the NBA, and showed up. The left the arena, left the game, and were left outside in the dark.

The section of Paul's letter to the Romans that we are focused on this week is Paul moving from the first section of his letter to a section, chapters 5-8, that focus on the powerful love of God that is found in Jesus Christ. In verse one, Paul declares that we are now at peace with God, through Christ. The peace Paul is referring to is not an "inner tranquility" (Witherington, pg. 133) or a healthy harmony that now exists for Christians. The word Paul uses here is similar to the Greek word dikaiothentes.

The peace Paul is referring to is a "restored or fixed relationship" (Witherington, pg. 133) between humanity and God. This new peace, our restored relationship now also offers us hope for the future. This hope for the future is grounder in the love God has shown to us through the Holy Spirit and Jesus Christ, which was made available by Christ's death for sinners.

It is enough to die for someone who is "good" but imagine dying for a sinner. What Paul is saying is that Christ's death for the sinner is not just a good idea or an arbitrary noble cause. Christ's death for the sinner is an invitation to us, those who gather on Sunday mornings in church, to embody the example of life that Christ gave to us. It's about living, not only about dying.

Jesus speaks of this invitation to sinners after he tells the chief priests and elders that prostitutes would make into the kingdom of heaven before anyone who believed them selves to be righteous. Jesus's parable of the wedding feast sets up for us the picture of one, who will enter into God's kingdom, and two, what it will take to enter into the kingdom.

"The kingdom of heaven may be compared to a king who gave a wedding banquet for his son. 3 He sent his slaves to call those who had been invited to the wedding banquet, but they would not come. 4 Again he sent other slaves, saying, 'Tell those who have been invited: Look, I have prepared my dinner, my oxen and my fat calves have been slaughtered, and everything is ready; come to the wedding banquet.' 5 But they made light of it and went away, one to his farm, another to his business, 6 while the rest seized his slaves, mistreated them, and killed them. 7 The king was enraged. He sent his troops, destroyed those murderers, and burned their city. 8 Then he said to his slaves, 'The wedding is ready, but those invited were not worthy. 9 Go therefore into the main streets, and invite everyone you find to the wedding banquet.' 10 Those slaves went out into the streets and gathered all whom they found, both good and bad; so the wedding hall was filled with guests.

11 "But when the king came in to see the guests, he noticed a man there who was not wearing a wedding robe, 12 and he said to him, 'Friend, how did you get in here without a wedding robe?' And he was speechless. 13 Then the king said to the attendants, 'Bind him hand and foot, and throw him into the outer darkness, where there will be

weeping and gnashing of teeth.' 14 For many are called, but few are chosen."

Here, what we learn is that it is not simply enough to show up for the party. That its not enough to put on the Miami Heat jersey. We received our wedding garments, out Miami Heat jersey, at our baptism. What we learn in this parable is that this is all about God's kingdom, a kingdom that as Paul tells in verse 11 that we are now reconciled with, and that we can be confident in that reconciliation because of Christ's life. And that is what grace and peace are all about. It's about building God's kingdom in here and now, grace is about the kingdom that no one wants.

The salvation offered to us through the Holy Spirit and the life of Christ is a *arrabon*, a down payment of what is to come through God's reconciled kingdom. Paul often speaks of salvation in the future tense, as in salvation is something that will come. But here Paul is saying the salvation is available to everyone, especially sinners or those on the outside, because of the way in which Christ lived, not exclusive to way in which Christ died. The grace that has been made available to us in the present is more than a gift.

The grace offered to us through Christ's death and his life offer us a reunion. Reunion with God but also with one another. A reunion that was not initially possible due our sinful nature. As theologian Stanley Hauerwas puts it, "grace is the reunion of life with life". The convent that was created between YHWH and the people of Israel was seen as a marriage bond, and since the covenant had been broken and a separation created reestablishment of the covenant/bond was necessary, and was carried about by the work of a Servant, resulting in a new creation.

We were created to be idols of God, and instead we have turned ourselves (just like those guests who refused to attend the wedding feast) into our own idols. Many protestants like to think that the grace and peace offered to us means that we are accepted. That we have our grace, which means that we have our salvation, which means that we are good to go when God's final judgement is made, which means we are good to go.

However, the wedding garment that we all wear because of our baptism calls us. We are called, because of our baptism and the grace offered to us, into the resurrection and the life of Jesus. This life calls for us to be different, to be a people who shine into the world so that the world might know that God's new kingdom is available in the present. Just like Paul is speaking in this part of his letter to the Romans of salvation, it is available here and now. Justification, in addition to making us right with God on a personal level, is to also transform us into people who do justice. It is our justification that makes us able to do justice. That justification enables us to wear our wedding garments, to put on our Heat jersey, and wear them as we engage in the grittiness of the world.

Because of the righteousness of Jesus, that is to say his obedience and faithfulness in His life and His death, we are can now be declared "right" before God and experience the *dikaioma*, or peace, that God has offered to us as a free gift. The end game to all of this, is that we get to inherit the age to come, God's kingdom and share that kingdom with those who are the "fair-weather" fans or who have simply never been invited to the game. Not only are we to be saved and justified before God through God's grace and through Jesus Christ, but we are to be the agents of God's renewed creation.

It is Christ's life that saves us, not Christ's death.
So grace does not mean that we have our wedding jacket on.

Romans 5:1-11 - The Elephant In The Room

Taylor Mertins

*Therefore, since we are justified by faith, we have peace with God
through our Lord Jesus Christ, through whom we have obtained access
to this grace in which we stand; and we boast in our hope of sharing
the glory of God. And not only that, but we also boast in our sufferings,
knowing that suffering produces endurance, and endurance produces
character, and character produces hope, and hope does not disappoint
us, because God's love has been poured into our hearts through the
Holy Spirit that has been given to us. For while we were still weak, at
the right time Christ died for the ungodly. Indeed, rarely will anyone
die for a righteous person – though perhaps for a good person someone
might actually dare to die. But God proves his love for us in that while
we still were sinners Christ died for us. Much more surely then, now
that we have been justified by his blood, will we be saved through him
from the wrath of God. For if while we were reconciled to God through
the death of his Son, much more surely, having been reconciled, will we
be saved by his life. But more than that, we even boast in God through
our Lord Jesus Christ, through whom we have now received
reconciliation. For while we were still weak, at the right time Christ
died for the ungodly.*

- Romans 5.1-11

Sometimes I'll be running at the gym, or walking the dog, or
just sitting in my office when an idea will pop into my head. The idea
starts like seed and then it germinates throughout my mind into sermon
topics and bible studies and blog posts. The idea grows and grows and
before it disappears into the gray matter of my brain I make sure to
write it down.

And, (would you believe it?) an idea is coming to me right now!
But I don't have any paper up here so I need you all to write this stuff
down (seriously).

Okay, we are justified by faith, God's faith in us. That's what we
talked about last week. And because we are justified by faith, we have

peace with God through Jesus. And, I mean, not only that, but we are bold to boast of God's grace in our worst moments, because we know that our suffering leads to endurance, and endurance leads to character, and character leads to hope.

Yeah, that's good.

We arrive at hope because God's love has been poured into our hearts through the Spirit. And we know that God loves us because while we were still weak, Christ died for the ungodly. Right? Like, how often will someone die for a righteous person? Though, I guess for a good person someone might actually dare to die. But God proves his love to us in that while we were sinners Christ died for us!

Still with me?

Okay, and its even more than that, now that we have been justified by Christ's blood we will be saved from the wrath of God. Through Jesus' death we were reconciled back to God, and through Jesus' life we will be saved! This is worth boasting about!

Did you get all of that?

Let me try to simplify in case I lost any of you: **We are justified by God's faith in us. Suffering leads to endurance, endurance to character, and character to hope. We arrive at this hope because we know God loves us. And we know God loves us because Christ died for us while we were yet sinners...**

Paul is hard to take from the pulpit. Give me one of the stories of Jesus' healings, or any of the parables; they preach themselves. **Sometimes I even think it would be better to just read the scripture and not preach anything at all.** But with Paul it takes on a new and strange and difficult dimension. Paul, in his letter to the Romans, writes in a form of rhetoric almost lost to the sands of time. **In our current age of 140 character tweets from our President, frenetic television shows, and fast-paced YouTube videos, we no longer have the minds, nor the time to hear Paul's theology.**

A theology that was probably dictated to someone else to write down while Paul was thinking it up.

You can almost hear that in the reading can't you? It's like he remembered something from a few sentences back and wants to clarify it.

The Epistle to the Romans is not a perfectly crafted sermon meant for pulpit proclamation. Instead, it's practical theology dictated from the greatest missionary the world has ever known.

Paul begins this section by addressing suffering; it's the part of the passage that is most often mentioned. And he's not just talking about some esoteric understanding of suffering. Paul is talking from experience! At the time of this letter, Paul was not a young, prematurely balding, healthy pastor standing in a pulpit telling his worn and suffering congregation to keep their chins up. No, this is entirely different. Paul suffered for the gospel, was arrested and persecuted, and yet he continued on. That's why he can say that suffering leads to hope. For Paul it's not a false and empty promise, it's what he has experienced.

And then we come to the section about dying for others.

Dying for others, for one's country, for our families, these stories captivate our hearts and our emotions. The thought of all the firefighters courageously rushing into the World Trade Center buildings on September 11th, or the countless volunteers who went to the other side of the world to fight in World War II, or just hearing about a mother who sacrifices herself to save her children, these stories really pull our heart strings.

But here, in Paul's letter to the Romans, this is even more radical than any of those stories. We have to try to put aside the emotional waves of grief and reverence for the stories of modern sacrifice for one's friends, family, or country. Paul does not say that Jesus died for his friends or his family or even his country.

Christ died for the ungodly!

Paul says that Christ died for us while we were his enemies!

Talk about an elephant in the room... **While we were yet sinners, Christ died for us.** We hear it in Romans, we hear it every time we come to the table for communion, but do we believe it?

We don't like talking about sin, we good Christian folk. We want to hear about love, peace, joy, hope, and happiness.

Only the converted, those whose lives have been truly captivated by Christ, think of themselves as sinners. Others won't have anything to do with it. That, my friends, is why we so seldom read from

Paul's letters in worship; we don't like the idea of ourselves as sinners, as ungodly.

"Preacher, can't you just give us a little more grace and love from the pulpit? Nobody wants to come to church to hear about sins!" And yet, we enjoy reading in the gossip columns and watching TMZ to learn about other people's sins, but that's their problem.

We don't like admitting our shortcomings, our faults, and our helplessness. We reject that gospel and substitute our own, one we talked about a couple weeks ago. We'd rather believe the American gospel: God helps those who help themselves. Actually, Paul tells us quite the opposite: When we could not help ourselves, when we were stuck in the shadow of sin, Christ died for us.

In our current age of tweets, twenty-minute TV shows, and traffic filled websites, we want everything compartmentalized as much as possible. Instead of reading a newspaper we want a short and brief email every morning that tells us only what we need to know. Instead of buying the latest hit book and spending an afternoon in our favorite chair, we read a summary online so we can talk about it with our friends. And instead of coming to church for an hour a week to experience the presence of God, people read the sermon online and check off the box on the Christian list of to-dos.

We, whether we admit it or not, are consumed by a desire to compress as much as possible into something as small as possible. Paul completely rejects this desire and notion that we can limit the gospel to any particular sentence or paragraph. **The Gospel, the Good News, is nothing less than the life, death, and resurrection of Jesus Christ, Son of Man, and Son of God.**

But, if we cannot resist the temptation, if we have to have something small, something we can keep with us at all times to know what the gospel is, this might work: **While we were still sinners, Christ died for the ungodly.**

This is crazy stuff people! Our Lord and Savior, the one in the stained glass window behind me, he died for the ungodly!

Who is the ungodliest person you can think of right now? I know some of you will immediately think of the members of ISIS who are terrorizing regions under their control. Others of you will immediately think of the leaders in North Korea who are trying their best to develop nuclear weapons of mass destruction. Some of you might think of Donald Trump and the seemingly endless Executive Orders streaming out of the Oval Office these days. Some of you might even be thinking about the person sitting in the pew next to you.

If it's too hard to think of someone ungodly, just think about one person you're angry with right now...

Jesus died for that person. Whoever you're thinking of, whoever that completely backwards and horrible and disappointing person is that's bouncing around in your mind right now, Jesus died for them.

That's the real elephant in the room. Jesus died precisely for the sort of person that would crucify him and mock him while they were doing it. People like us.

These things we call faith and discipleship are not very religious in the sense of being pretty and easy to handle. They are not something we can carry around in our pockets during the week only to show up when we need them. **The cross of Christ is far too offensive to be religious.**

The cross and the death of Christ shatter our expectations given to us by the world. They, in all their strangeness, reorient us back toward the radical nature of God's love. The offensive and scandalous cross is our paradoxical hope and joy. **Because in and through the cross, God did something that none of us would do.**

As the old hymn goes, the immortal God hath died for me.

God's love in Christ is so comprehensive and so bewildering that it is able to wash away even the greatest of sins.

We started this sermon with a dictation, an imaginative way to reimagine the writing of Paul's letter to the Romans. If you wrote down anything I hope you wrote this: While we were yet sinners God died for the ungodly, for us.

Now I want you to write down the name of the person you thought of just a moment ago, the person who you're angry with. Write his or her name at the top as if you meant to send this letter to them.

Now you know that I'm going to ask you to send it. And I know that you probably won't. You won't for the same reason I wouldn't; it's offensive and it's uncomfortable. We won't send this affirmation of God's unnerving love to someone else because it would force us into an area we'd rather avoid; we don't want to come off as too evangelistic, or too churchy. We don't want to admit our sin.

Can you imagine the shock on the person's face if they received your dictated letter from the adapted words of the apostle Paul? Can you picture how bewildered they would be by something Christians say all the time? Can you imagine how it would change the way you look at them for the rest of your days?

While we were still weak, Christ died for the ungodly. In our weakness we reject the challenge to confront our sins and we reject the forgiving nature of God's love for the world. We forget that Christ died for our shame and our sin and our sadness. We forget that Christ died for our disappointment and our degenerate derelictions and our deficiencies. We forget that Christ died for us and for the people whose names' are at the top of our letters.

And yet Christ still died for us! What wondrous love in this that that caused the Lord of bliss to bear the dreadful curse for my soul! To God and to the Lamb who is the great I am, we shall sing! And when from death we're free, and through eternity, we shall sing.

For while we were yet sinners, Christ died for us.
Amen.

Romans 5:12-21 - Stuck In The Bushes

Taylor Mertins

Therefore, just as sin came into the world through one man, and death came through sin, and so death spread to all because all have sinned – sin was indeed in the world before the law, but sin is not reckoned when there is no law. Yet death exercised dominion from Adam to Moses, even over those whose sins were not like the transgression of Adam, who is a type of the one who was to come. But the free gift is not like the trespass. For if the many died through the one man's trespass, much more surely have the grace of God and the free gift in the grace of the one man, Jesus Christ, abounded for the many. And the free gift is not like the effect of the one man's sin. For the judgment following one trespass brought condemnation, but the free gift following many trespasses brings justification. If, because of the one man's trespass, death exercised dominion through that one, much more surely will those who receive the abundance of grace and the free gift of righteousness exercise dominion in the life through the one man, Jesus Christ. Therefore just as one man's trespass led to condemnation for all, so one man's act of righteousness leads to justification and life for all. For just as by the one man's disobedience the many were made sinners, so by the one man's obedience the many will be made righteous. But law came in, with the result that the trespass multiplied; but where sin increased, grace abounded all the more, so that, just as sin exercised dominion in death, so grace might also exercise dominion in death, so grace might also exercise dominion through justification leading to eternal life through Jesus Christ our Lord. But law came in, with the result that the trespass multiplied; but where sin increased, grace abounded all the more.

- Romans 5.12-21

I take a lot of pride in my ability to communicate with people of different age groups. On any given week I will spend time explaining theology to five year olds in our preschool, fifteen year olds in our youth group, 50 year olds in our bible study, and then the rest of you on Sunday morning. It is definitely a challenge taking ideas from the likes of Paul and proclaiming them in a way that can be appreciated for the here and now for the young and old.

But sometimes, I fail.

Like the time I tried to address the moral and ethical dilemmas of Capital Punishment to our youth group one night, to the times I've tried to proclaim the strange complexity of confronting our finitude on Ash Wednesday to our preschoolers, to the times I've told some of our much older adults that one must have the faith of a child to inherit the kingdom of God.

Communicating the gospel, sharing the Good News, is a challenge, and I definitely failed once when we were on our mission trip to West Virginia a couple summers back. **Picture it, if you can: It is hotter than blazes outside, and I'm stuck in a tiny kitchen surrounded by teenagers who would rather be instagramming and snap chatting one another than cleaning a floor or painting a ceiling. And it was silent.**

So I did what I do: I started asking questions...

"What's your favorite story from the bible?"

One of our boys immediately said something about David defeating Goliath. The Davidic story will forever rest in the hearts of prepubescent boys who struggle with how rapidly the girls are growing while they remain the same.

A boy from another church said, "Well, I kinda like the one about, you know, Jesus feeding people?" while saliva poured out of his mouth as he stared at the cooler in the corner filled with our lunches.

A girl from a different church said, "I've always been rather captivated by Jesus turning water into wine at the wedding at Cana in Galilee." To which I made a mental note to bring this up with her youth group later in the evening. No sensible teenage girl should be thinking about water turning into wine, and certainly not when Jesus has anything to do with it.

We went on and on, and then it was my turn to answer. "Well" I said, "It's not my favorite story, but I've always loved this little detail at the beginning of the bible, in the book of Genesis. Adam and Eve were placed in the Garden of Eden with a choice. They could choose to live in perfect harmony with God and God's creation, with each other, free from sin and free from death. But Adam and Eve made the wrong choice, they wanted to be like God, and as soon as they tasted the fruit from the tree of knowledge of Good and Evil, their eyes were opened, and they knew they were naked.

"But here's the part that gets me every time. Almost as soon as they sin, they heard the sound of God walking in the garden and they both sprinted for the bushes. But God called out, 'Where are you Adam? Where are you Eve?' After waiting for a few moments, Adam popped his little head out of the bushes, and told God that he was hiding because he was naked and afraid."

To which God said, **'Who told you that you were naked?'**

"Isn't that hilarious?" – The teenagers had all stopped working while I was sharing the story, and now they were all staring at me with eyebrows askew. I could hear the paint dripping off their brushes onto the floor as if even the crickets were too concerned to chirp. One of the boys finally broke the silence to say, "Um… I don't think it's very funny. If I were naked and God came looking for me, I'd run for the bushes too!"

Do we know this old, old, story? Do we know what sin is? Do we know what happened to Adam and Eve in the Garden of Eden?

What kind of stories and habits and beliefs do we want to pass on to the coming generations? I feel like I am forever hearing about the good ol' days when "we knew our bibles" and "we would've gone to school with snow like this when I was a kid" and "we entertained ourselves with our imaginations and not a screen in our pockets."

Do we wish that things could go back to the way they were? Are we worried about the future that we are handing to our children?

We can talk and talk about what we want to pass on, what we hope to engender, but if we don't know our story, if we don't know where we came from, how in the world can we even hope to take a step in the right direction?

Just as sin came into the world through one man… Paul assumes that we know the story, that we know the details of the Garden. He does not waste lines in his letter rehashing the characters and the questions, he gets right to the point: Sin came into the world through Adam and Eve. They, and therefore we, broke the covenant with God. The transition from God's rule to the rule of sin and death came into the world because of our rebellious and disobedient desires.

This is our condition. There is no going back. Fear and shame and anger and disappointment are our lives. We are, in a sense, stuck in the bushes for good, hoping that God will not come looking for us.

We are in the bushes. And Lent is a great time to ask the question: Why? Which of the commandments have we broken? Did we work on the Sabbath? Have we hated our mothers or our fathers? Did we covet something that did not belong to us? An object, a job, or God forbid, a person?

How would we respond if we heard God walking toward us in the middle of our sin? **We, like Adam and like that boy on the mission trip, would run for the bushes.**

Paul assumes that we know the story of Adam and Eve in the Garden because it is OUR story! Adam's sin is our sin, and it not only divided us from God, but also brought death into the world, which spread like a disease. This is Paul's point, and he says it in these few verses over and over again.

We are trapped in sin and death and we are stuck in the bushes. That's the story of the Garden. Is this what we want to pass on?

Truly I tell you, we cannot know who we are to be, if we do not know our story. This inexhaustible, unexplainable, indescribable moment from the beginning is who we are. It is the story of how the life of order fell into disorder. **But, thanks be to God, it is not the end of the story.**

Adam brought the entirety of humanity down, down to the depths of death and destruction. Jesus, however, is the new way who is able to create a new humanity.

The promise of a good and remade and hopeful future comes from the old story that is forever new. The story of our death, and then the death that freed us from sin and death.

In Jesus Christ our stories are made new; God, as the author of salvation, takes up the pen and starts a new chapter through the life, death, and resurrection of his son. This is the story that those who are coming, the one who will follow us, need to hear. This is the story we need to share. We need to pray for the courage to shout this story from the rooftops as if our lives depended on it, because they do.

The only way to victory, the way to upend what was done in the Garden, is through the cross. We might think of a different way, a more efficient and less taxing way, but the way of the cross is the WAY that Christ defeated death.

But this is not an easy story to tell. The message and value of the cross comes with a cost. It is difficult, it is selfless, and frankly it is un-American. Today, we would rather surround the young with lessons that teach very different values: get the job, earn as much as you can, find the right spouse, buy the car, lose the weight, invest in the right companies, bring 2.5 children into the world, purchase the perfect house, and you will be free and life will be perfect.

That's the story we tell. **And it's a lie! It's all a lie! None of these things can give life. They cannot give us the identity and purpose and hope we so desire. The job will change, the money will disappear, the spouse will grow old, the body will too, the companies will falter, the car will rust, the children will not listen; Sin and Death corrupt them all.**

But there is nevertheless Good News, there is a way out of the bondage that was brought into the world by the one we call Adam. We are freed through the one we call Christ.

We are stuck in the bushes of our own sin and shame. But Christ comes to us in the Garden of our own demise without a question, but a call. Jesus does not ask us who told us we were sinning, **Jesus says follow me. Follow me to Galilee, follow me to Gethsemane, follow me to Calvary.**

Jesus is the way and the truth and the life. Sin has increased in this world and in our lives, but God's grace in Jesus Christ has abounded all the more.

The story, our story, began in the Garden, but it did not end there. It continued through the strange and wild wilderness in the days of Abraham, weaved through the journey to Egypt and back again in Jacob and Joseph. It rose through the power of David and Solomon, and fell through the failure of God's people worshipping idols. It danced through the prophets who remained faithful to the Lord, it endured droughts and famines, it saw suffering and sadness. It connected the lives of the powerful with the powerless, it brought down the high and lifted up the lowly.

It was born again in a manger in a small town called Bethlehem; it trudged through the towns of Galilee and sailed over the sea. It walked through the streets of Jerusalem and turned over the tables at the Temple. It was dragged before the council and the ruling elite. It was marched up to a hill and nailed to a cross. It was silent in a tomb for three days. And it broke free from the chains of sin and death.

That is the story. It is a story worth telling over and over again; because in it we discover who we are and whose we are. In it we see ourselves stuck in the bushes being beckoned by Jesus to follow him. And in it we realize that it is not just *a* story, nor even *our* story, but *THE* story. Amen.

Romans 5:12-21 - Feel the Bern

Jason Micheli

Therefore, just as sin came into the world through one man, and death came through sin, and so death spread to all because all have sinned—sin was indeed in the world before the law, but sin is not reckoned when there is no law. Yet death exercised dominion from Adam to Moses, even over those whose sins were not like the transgression of Adam, who is a type of the one who was to come. But the free gift is not like the trespass. For if the many died through the one man's trespass, much more surely have the grace of God and the free gift in the grace of the one man, Jesus Christ, abounded for the many. And the free gift is not like the effect of the one man's sin. For the judgment following one trespass brought condemnation, but the free gift following many trespasses brings justification. If, because of the one man's trespass, death exercised dominion through that one, much more surely will those who receive the abundance of grace and the free gift of righteousness exercise dominion in life through the one man, Jesus Christ. Therefore just as one man's trespass led to condemnation for all, so one man's act of righteousness leads to justification and life for all. For just as by the one man's disobedience the many were made sinners, so by the one man's obedience the many will be made righteous. But law came in, with the result that the trespass multiplied; but where sin increased, grace abounded all the more, so that, just as sin exercised dominion in death, so grace might also exercise dominion through justification leading to eternal life through Jesus Christ our Lord.

—Romans 5.12-21

I know most of you don't want to hear about politics from the pulpit. As one of you commented in all-caps hysteria about one of our dialogue sermons this spring: "KEEP POLITICS OUT OF THE PULPIT. STICK TO THE GOSPEL!!! :("

Look, I get it. But what the Hell am I supposed to do when politics and the Gospel collide through no fault of my own?

For example, the otherwise low-profile confirmation hearing on Capitol Hill last week for Russell Vought, President Trump's nominee to be deputy director of something-something.

A sleepy session on CSPAN raised eyebrows and spawned social media memes when Sanders turned the Bern on Russell Vought and, literally wagging his finger, shouted: "Do you think that people who are not Christians are condemned?

Sanders did not relent his inquisition: "Do you believe people in the Muslim religion stand condemned?" "What about Jews? Do they stand condemned, too?"

Russell Vought, repeatedly, responded: "I'm a Christian."

To which Bernie raised his voice and bellowed at the nominee: "I understand you are a Christian, but there are other people who have different religions in this country and around the world. In your judgment, do you think that people who are not Christians are condemned?"

Behind Bernie's soapbox assault was a blog post Russell Vought wrote a year ago in support of his evangelical alma mater, Wheaton College.

Wheaton had suspended a tenured professor whose views contradicted the school's statement of faith and, during the ensuing controversy, Vought weighed in that "all are condemned apart from Jesus Christ."

After wagging his finger, Bernie threw up his hands at Vought's professed belief in the centrality of Jesus Christ for salvation and declared that his faith claims disqualified him from serving his country through civil service.

Now I'd be a liar if I said the prospect of someone being disqualified from serving in the Trump administration because they were too Christian didn't amuse me.

I think it would be hilarious if more Christians were disqualified from serving the Donald.

But my delight in that prospect aside, Wheaton College's Statement of Faith isn't substantively different than the confessions of any other Christian tradition.

———

Wheaton College might put it differently than the United Methodist Church, but neither Wheaton nor Vought said anything contrary to what we say when we recite in the Apostles Creed: "I believe in Jesus Christ his *only* Son our Lord…who will come again to *judge*…"

Look, I admit I'm no fan of Bernie Sanders.

When you're a pastor in the Mainline Protestant Church you're already exposed to more self-righteousness than you can take.

I'm not a Bernie fan—I have room in my life for only one socialist Jew.

I'm no Bernie fan, but what caught my attention about this story wasn't what Sanders said to Vought but what Christians said in response to Sanders, to Bernie's inflammatory rhetoric.

Russell Moore of the Southern Baptist Convention pointed to the Bible: "Christians don't believe that we are constructing our faith. We believe that it's been handed to us by God."

Okay. That's true.

Still Christians bypassed the creeds and pointed to the Constitution and the manner in which Bernie's religious prejudice violated the Constitution's religious protection.

Again, that's true even if it's a tepid *Christian* response.

Vought himself said he believes "that all individuals are made in the image of God and are worthy of dignity and respect regardless of their religious beliefs."

That's vanilla and generic but still, it's correct.

But I'm surprised those were the only types of answers offered by Christians.

———

"Do you think that people who are not Christians stand condemned? I'm a Jew, do you believe I am condemned as well?"

Bernie asked.

And of course, the simple answer, the straight-up answer, the direct and unambiguous answer, the Gospel which Russell Vought and Russell Moore and Pope Francis and Mother Theresa and the Apostle Paul all proclaim—the answer is 'Yes.'

Yes, you stand condemned.

Yes, they stand condemned.

And so do I. I stand condemned.

And so do you.

These days there's a lot of talk about the decline of churches in America, but maybe we should be more concerned with the decline in church members' ability to articulate the Gospel.

Or maybe the latter produces the former. Maybe the church has waned alongside church members' ability to articulate the Gospel message that all of us — _all_ of us — stand condemned.

All have sinned.

Not one of us is righteous — Jew, Muslim, Christian; Religious or Secular — not one of is right in God's eyes by anything we do or believe.

No matter what Bernie thinks, that's not an exclusive belief; you literally cannot get more inclusive than the Gospel message that all of us are sinners.

All stand condemned.

————

The Apostle Paul continues his argument by widening his frame here in Romans 5.

In order to comprehend fully that your justification is not about anything you do, Paul needs you to understand that 'sin' is about more than something you do and accrue.

Sin, Paul wants you to see, is a Power with a capital P.

It's Sin, Paul wants you to grasp, with a capital S.

Paul doesn't use the word sin as a verb, as something we do.

Sin is instead the subject of verbs.

Paul speaks of Sin not as something we do but as a Something that does — not simply an act we commit but as an Agency that conscripts. and implicates every last one of us, religious and irreligious.

First, Paul personifies all of us, the entire human community, as Adam, but then notice how Paul mirrors that by personifying Sin and Death — personifying them as reigning monarchs:

Sin won lordship over all humanity and Death came through Sin, and so Death advanced through all the world like an invading army.

You see, Death for Paul is not natural nor is it the punishment that follows Adam's sin.

Death, for Paul, is a partner with Sin—Sin with a capital S—and it's not until the end of his letter to the Romans that you discover both Sin and Death are synonymous for him with the Power of Satan.

Sin, Death, Satan—they're all interchangeable terms.

Death, for Paul, is a rival anti-god Power that snuck into God's creation through Adam's disobedience.

Sin and Death, for Paul, are Pharaohs that enslave us.

Actually instead of Pharaoh the word Paul uses is *kurios*.

It's the same word Paul uses to refer to Jesus here in Romans 5:

Just as Sin exercised lordship in Death, so Grace might also exercise lordship through justification leading to eternal life through Jesus Christ our Kurios.

The lordship of Sin and Death vs. the lordship of Jesus Christ: it's an intentional contrast.

What Paul wants you to see is that the Gospel is about a battle between contending Powers, a Power that would bind us versus a Power that would set us free.

And if that language sounds primitive and mythological to you, then talk to an alcoholic or someone addicted to drugs or porn or racism.

Talk to someone whose family is stuck perpetuating generations of abuse and antagonism.

I've been here long enough to know there are folks like that all around you this morning.

They'll tell you: Paul's 'mythological' language matches real world experience.

You don't even need to believe in a literal, historical 'Adam' to nod your head to Paul here because the truth of what Paul writes here in Romans 5 is all over the headlines: from Columbine to Sandy Hook to Steve Scalise this week.

What better way to explain it than to say, like Paul, Sin is an enslaving lord that holds all of us captive, such that we cannot *improve* ourselves much less deliver ourselves.

When Christ comes into the world, he comes into occupied territory, and when you come into the world you do too.

All of us are sinners because none of us can choose to live elsewhere.

We're all slaves to the Power of Sin.

But we're accomplices too.

We're captives, that's true, but we're culpable as well.

We're culpable too.

Again, the truth of that is all over the headlines:

> Columbine — Sandy Hook — Monroe Avenue.
> Michael Brown — Sandra Bland — Philando Castile.
> Ground Zero — Paris — Orlando — Nice — London

A Power that is not God has got us.

But we're guilty too.

All of us. All stand condemned.

Just so it sinks in, Paul repeats it 7 times in chapter 5.

Over and over and over and over and over and over and over:

One man's trespass led to condemnation for all.
— — — — — — — —-

During Russell Vought's Senate confirmation hearing, Bernie kept getting on his soapbox to ask Russell Vought what he believed about other religions, as though Christianity is but one religion among many in America.

But there's where Bernie's wrong because if you understand Paul's message, then you understand that Christianity, at its core, is not religious at all.

Look it up in the dictionary. The definitions of religion are all about us. The definitions of religion are all about what we do to seek God: belief and prayer and practice.

Disciplines we use to connect to God.

But Paul's message is that God helps those who cannot help themselves. Paul's whole irreligious point here is summed up in God's first words after Adam's sin: "Adam, where are you?"

The simple answer to Bernie's question is 'Yes.'

———

Yes, you stand condemned.

And so do I.

As all are in Adam, under the lordship of Sin and Death, all stand condemned.

But to leave the answer there is to mistake Paul's message of justification for something we do.

Because of one man's sin, all stand condemned...But, Paul says —Paul's big buts always signal the good news—*another man's rectification of that sin means life for all.*

In Adam *all* stand condemned, **but** through the obedience that is the blood of the New Adam, God declares *all* of us 'Not Guilty.'

That's good news.

But it's only part of it.

The Christian hope, Paul's Gospel, the good news of justification is even bigger.

It's the news that in Jesus Christ God has appeared in enemy territory not simply to forgive but to free.

Not only does this free gift of God in Jesus Christ make you no longer culpable, if you trust it—if you but put your faith in it—it can make you no longer captive as well.

"Not guilty" are just the first two words of this good news.

Because the righteous blood of Jesus Christ exchanged for your own not only acquits you of your culpability in the ultimate courtroom it can, if you put your trust in it, set you on the path to be freed.

Freed from the bonds of the Captor, whom Paul calls here: Sin and Death.

The Gospel isn't just that in Jesus Christ you have been declared "Not Guilty." The Gospel is that you can be declared Not You.

The Gospel is that in Jesus Christ, in Jesus Christ *alone*, in Jesus Christ our *only* Savior, you can become a New You.

By faith.

And that's where Bernie might not like my answer, but I know it to be true, not only because the Bible tells me so but because I've seen it for myself.

You will never be a new you on your own.

On your own, every new you will turn out to be another old Adam.

Jesus Christ is the only New Adam able to create a new humanity, in his story your stories of guilt and shame, your cracks and your captivity can be re-narrated. Re-told.

Receive this free gift in faith and the other half of the Gospel is yours:

> You can be re-made.
> Not just forgiven but set free.
> Not only justified but rectified.

Bernie won't like the rest of the answer.

But there *is* only one Savior because there is only one — only one — who was not born into the dominion of Adam, into the lordship of Sin and Death.

Jesus Christ our Lord.

Romans 6:1-11 - On Using Bad Words In Church

Taylor Mertins

What then are we to say? Should we continue in sin in order that grace may abound? By no means! How can we who died to sin go on living in it? Do you not know that all of us who have been baptized into Christ Jesus were baptized into his death? Therefore we have been buried with him by baptism into death, so that, just as Christ was raised from the dead by the glory of the Father, so we too might walk in newness of life. For if we have been united with him in a death like his, we will certainly be united with him in a resurrection like his. We know that our old self was crucified with him so that the body of sin might be destroyed, and we might no longer be enslaved to sin. But if we have died with Christ, we believe that we will also live with him. We know that Christ, being raised from the dead, will never die again; death no longer has dominion over him. The death he died, he died to sin, once for all; but the life he lives, he lives to God. So you also must consider yourselves dead to sin and alive to God in Christ Jesus. What then are we to say? Should we continue in sin in order that grace may abound? By no means!

- Romans 6.1-11

What's the worst word you can imagine hearing from the pulpit? In a world where you can get away with saying and doing just about anything, is the church still a sacred place untainted by the desires of the world? There are plenty of strange and difficult and downright awful stories from scripture that we can read from the lectern, but don't you think the pulpit should remain nice and clean?

During the season of Lent, we confront our finitude, our sinfulness, and our total dependence on the Lord. It is a tough time for us comfortable Christians, because these are exactly the types of things that many of us would rather avoid.

Gone are the days when we could expect to hear about sin and be challenged and convicted out of it. Gone are the days when we could affirm our finite lives without needing the stark reminder of ashes on our foreheads once a year.

Today, God has been reduced to a bumper-stickered and hallmarked version of love. Nothing more, nothing less, nothing else.

Today, church is not the place for judgment and for talk about sin. Regardless of their primacy in scripture, we would all be happier if we could avoid them.

The same holds true for foul language.

Right?

This is definitely not the place for someone like me to stand in front of people like you and use words that are forbidden from the radio and are relegated to rated-R movies.

As I heard someone say recently, **"Preacher, there are just some things you don't talk about it church."**

There is a seemingly endless list of things not to talk about in church; **things like politics, abortion, divorce, war, sex, taxes, just to name a few. But foul language, language that results in soap-in-the-mouth discipline, is a particularly poignant thing to avoid in church.**

And I have a friend in ministry who has completely ignored this accepted fact.

He loves to use foul language from the pulpit. Whether it's the Christmas Eve sermon and the church is filled with young families who only show up for one worship service a year, or an Ash Wednesday service where only the die-hard Christians come out, he's known for his colorful language. He'll tell you that he uses those particular words in order to enhance the sermon in such a way that it will become more memorable and hit closer to home.

And a lot of the people at his church can't stand it.

"Why does he feel like he has to resort to such awful language?" "The church deserves better than this." "Does he talk to his mother that way?"

And, I think, they have a point. When the language used becomes more memorable or more important than what is being proclaimed, something has fallen a part. For instance: His recent Ash Wednesday sermon was titled "God Doesn't Give A @#$%" I read it and listened to it online, it was phenomenal. The theology and the proclamation were remarkably faithful to the One who is faithful to us. But a few of the people from the church called me afterward and couldn't even begin to express what the sermon was about at all; they were still hung up on the title.

However, there is a value to using some bad words in church.

During the season of Lent, this time after Epiphany but before Easter, there is a specific word that we avoid at all costs. It's really bad. The word is… well, I'm not supposed to say it. Um, how can I do this…

Okay, there's this great song by Ray Stevens called the Mississippi Squirrel Revival, maybe you've heard it, and part of it goes like this: The day the squirrel went berserk // In the First Self-Righteous Church // In the sleepy little town of Pascagoula // It was a fight for survival // That broke out in revival // They were jumpin' pews and shoutin' @#$%^&*!"

You know the word I'm talking about? You might not have even noticed it, but we have not said the "H" word in worship since before Ash Wednesday. It has not been read from the lectern, it has not been hidden in one of the verses from our hymns, and I certainly haven't used it from the pulpit.

We purposely avoid the word during Lent so that when we shout it out on Easter it will mean all that much more. We specifically deprive ourselves of this important and powerful word to create a longing for the realization of all that the life, death, and resurrection of Jesus promises to us and to the world.

And there's another bad "H" word that we need to talk about: **Hell.**

I don't mean the place filled with fire and a red-toned, frighteningly tall, horned figure with a trident and a bifurcated tail. I mean using "hell" as an expression.

Paul writes: "What then are we to say? Should we continue in sin in order that grace may abound? By no means!" Now, what I'm about to say will probably get me in trouble, but so be it. That little ending, the "by no means" just doesn't cut it. In Greek the expression is "me genotio" and it is way more emphatic than "by no means." Some translations have it as "God forbid" or "Definitely not" but even both of those miss the mark.

In what we read last week, Paul wrote: **"When sin increased, grace abounded all the more." And it's as if Paul knew that people would hear those words and say, "Dude, that's awesome! If grace abounds all the more when sin increases, then lets keep the sins rolling!"**

And here is Paul's response: "Should we continue to sin in order that grace may abound? **HELL NO!**"

Our lives have changed forever. We can't just retreat to the ways of the past because grace abounds. God in Christ has made in us a new creation! The gift of God in Christ on the cross was, and is, such that we are forever freed from the tyranny of sin and death. Should we continue to sin in order that grace may abound? **HELL NO!**

But that's not the last bad word we're going to talk about today. No, we still need to talk about "Sin" and "Death." Perhaps two of the worst words that can ever be used in church. And you can tell they're bad word precisely because of how rarely they are used in a place like this.

We need to talk about these bad words, not because they are normal parts of human experience, but because they are false powers that rule over us. That's how Paul understood them: Sin *reigns*, Death has *dominion*.

You need only turn on the television for five minutes in the evening to see how true this really is: The nighty News hour is filled to the brim with the failures and faults and sins of other people; The Republican Party failed to procure their dream for American Healthcare. Left Wing activists went on a violent strike in another major city. Augusta County citizen receives life sentence for horrible crime. North Korea has another failed missile test but they are getting closer to developing their own weapons of mass destruction. The market fluctuated with each tweet from our president. Test scores have fallen in local school leading to speculation that it will close… **All of them are negative.**

And then when they go to a commercial break we are bombarded by products designed to make us believe that we can and will live forever; Use this cream and your wrinkles will disappear.

Invest in this company and you will never have to worry about money. Go on this vacation and you will feel happy and healthy like the people running on the beach or tanning by the pool.

We live under the tyranny of sin and death. But Paul says this should not be so!

We who have been baptized into Christ have been crucified with Christ. Our sinful selves are put to death on the Cross so that we will no longer be slaves to the bad words of Sin and Death.

Long ago, we would have known this without Paul having to remind us. Baptisms, long ago, were all about death. That's where the Baptists beat us today, I'm sorry to say. **When the Baptists baptize, they fully submerge people under water. And, depending on the faithfulness of the pastor, the soon-to-be-new Christian might be held under for quite a long time.**

You would've missed the baptism to death if you were with us in Alexandria when Elijah was baptized. No, we didn't hold him under a tub of water to embody the death to sin. No, we didn't give him some old and tattered gown to wear. Elijah looked perfect in his little khakis, and button-up shirt, and bow-tie, and mustard-colored cardigan. Elijah was sprinkled with water, and the perfectly portioned amount of holy oil was smeared in the shape of the cross on his forehead. And, he was carried out to the congregation and held up high by the same preacher who curses too much.

We miss the death to sin in our baptisms. But we have a member of our lectionary bible study who really gets it. Judy had avoided church for decades before God grabbed her by the heart and said, "Follow me." She brought her questions and her doubts to her preacher, and after a time she felt her heart strangely warmed and felt moved to be baptized.

Unlike babes in the United Methodist Church, Judy marched up to the giant baptismal font and prepared to jump into the all-too-cold water. And outside, through the multicolored stained glass windows, a thunderstorm was brewing.

Judy slowly descended into the water, and with cracks of thunder in the distance the preacher plunged her into the depths of death to sin. I like to imagine that if she opened her eyes underwater, even for the briefest of moments, she would have seen a flash of lighting that illuminated the entire congregation. **The whole moment felt as if the rule of Sin and Death, the dominion of the devil himself, was making one final dash to keep her under their control. But alas, the grace of Jesus Christ abounded all the more, and she arose from the water dead to sin and death.**

Are we to continue in sin that grace may abound? **HELL NO!**

God has changed us! Not just through the waters of our baptisms, not just through the bread that we break and the cup from which we drink, but also through the death of Jesus on the cross. It changes everything! This gift transforms our very lives to the point that we should feel compelled not to fall back into the old ways, to the old self, ruled by Sin and Death.

But we know the truth: we do fall back. We know that those who are sent to prison for horrible crimes have an all too high likelihood of returning one day. We know that those caught in adultery tend to habitually cheat for the rest of their lives. We know that even the strongest member of an AA group can fall off the wagon.

We know that we fall back.

We say "never again" to so many thing only to have them come right back around. We say never again to the anger, to the cigarette, to the bottle, to the cheating, to the lying, to the hatred, to the racism, to the homophobia, to the elitism, to the narcissism, to defeatism, to a great number of things.

They never stop.

The fact that they never stop is evidence of the power of Sin in this world, which reigns in Death.

But our lives have been changed! God has wiped away the old self and clothed us with the new. God washed away our insecurities and insufficiencies and said, "My grace is enough." God was nailed to the hard wood of the cross to die a death that we might die in our baptism. God was raised from the dead as we were brought forth from the water to live a resurrected and holy life.

The death Jesus died, he died to sin, once for all; but the life he lives, he lives to God. So we also must consider ourselves dead to sin and alive to God in Christ Jesus our Lord.

Should we continue in sin in order that grace may abound? **HELL NO!** Amen.

Romans 7:14-25 - The Worm at the Core of the Apple

Jason Micheli

For we know that the law is spiritual; but I am of the flesh, sold into slavery under sin. I do not understand my own actions. For I do not do what I want, but I do the very thing I hate. Now if I do what I do not want, I agree that the law is good. But in fact it is no longer I that do it, but sin that dwells within me. For I know that nothing good dwells within me, that is, in my flesh. I can will what is right, but I cannot do it. For I do not do the good I want, but the evil I do not want is what I do. Now if I do what I do not want, it is no longer I that do it, but sin that dwells within me. So I find it to be a law that when I want to do what is good, evil lies close at hand. For I delight in the law of God in my inmost self, but I see in my members another law at war with the law of my mind, making me captive to the law of sin that dwells in my members. Wretched man that I am! Who will rescue me from this body of death? Thanks be to God through Jesus Christ our Lord! So then, with my mind I am a slave to the law of God, but with my flesh I am a slave to the law of sin.

—Romans 7.14-25

"I'd seen women who admitted to having an abortion receive forgiveness, and I'd noticed how women who had kept their babies seemed somehow harder to forgive. But the more I thought about abortion, the more I knew I couldn't go through with it. In my view, abortion is taking a life that belongs to God alone, and I couldn't do that. I chose what I believed to be the good; I didn't know all this would follow from my decision."

Maybe you read the story in the *Washington Post* a few weeks ago. Or maybe you caught it on CBS, Fox, or CNN (FAKE NEWS).

Maddi Runkles, soon to be a freshman at Bob Jones University, is an 18-year-old graduate of Heritage Academy, a private Christian high school in Frederick, Maryland.

She's also in her second trimester and due in the fall.

According to her own first-person account in the *Washington Post*, Maddi Runkles was a straight A student at Heritage Academy.

She sported a 4.0 GPA and she played forward on the school soccer team. She was president of the Student Council and vice-president of the Key Club.

She volunteered every Sunday in her Baptist Church's nursery and taught at Vacation Bible School every summer. Maddi was by her own testimony an over-achieving, brown-nosing, not just a good but a *perfect* student.

She out-Wobegoned all the children of Lake Wobegone. She was successful at everything except one.

She failed to keep her chastity pledge.

She was born again and soon to give birth.

When Maddi Runkles confessed her secret to her parents late this winter, they bucked the stereotype of conservative Christian parents. They did not scorn their daughter. Her Dad even told her: "God is in this somewhere with you and we'll be with you too."

Before you smile and tear up, let me tell you about her school.

As word of Maddi's sin got out, Heritage Academy convened their school board for an emergency meeting where they moved to strip Maddi of all her leadership positions in the student body.

They kicked her off the soccer team. They suspended her. They even told her she could not attend her younger brother's baseball games.

They didn't hand her a big, fat red *A* for her letter jacket, but they did they ban her from campus *until after* she delivered her baby.

The school board even called a school-wide student assembly where Maddi confessed her transgression to her peers, expressed repentance, and asked for their forgiveness.

Nevertheless, the school board informed Maddi that while they would permit her to receive her diploma, they would not allow her to walk with her classmates at the graduation ceremony.

That was the straw.

The board's decision to exclude Maddi from her graduation provoked a public outcry, which emboldened Maddi's family to fight the graduation ban.

When Maddi's story went viral and the school started to receive mocking press coverage, her community's reflex was to protect the school.

Eventually, her community turned on her, making the Runkles family the object of nasty emails, inflammatory social media posts, rude remarks in public, and dangerous threats in private.

Some of Maddi's friends from Heritage Academy, seeing their school in danger, said she was spoiled and seeking publicity.

They slut-shamed her.

They attend bible class at Heritage Academy for an hour every school day.

In a letter to the parents, the principal of Heritage Academy wrote that Maddi was "being disciplined not because she is pregnant but because she is immoral...the best way to love her- (pay attention to the words) the good we can do for her right now- is to hold her accountable for her morality that began this situation."

The best way to love her...the good we can do for her.

According to the *New York Times*, Maddi Runkles keeps an ultrasound photo of her baby on her nightstand. It's a boy. She refers to him as a "blessing."

Nevertheless, Maddi confessed to the reporter:

"I chose life. I chose (pay attention to the words) the good, but now that I see what my decision has produced . . . sometimes it feels like it wasn't worth it."

For that very reason, that Maddi Runkles would even entertain regret over what she believed had been the good and right act of not seeking an abortion, pro-life organizations like March for Life and Students for Life rallied to her side.

As Jeanne Mancini, President of March for Life, pointed out to the *Post*:

"In the manner they held Maddi accountable, Heritage Academy, a vigorously anti-abortion school, has made it more likely that future students like Maddi will choose to have an abortion."

———

The theologian Karl Barth said that preachers should approach the pulpit with the Bible in one hand and the *New York Times* in the other.

What Barth meant was that the world, as its described in the Good News of the Gospel, becomes clearer to see when you find it confirmed by and corroborated in the pages of your newspaper.

Here's what readers of both the newspaper and today's scripture text should ask:

- In choosing the good of carrying her baby to term, did Maddi Runkles seek to split her school and community apart?
- In holding Maddi accountable did Heritage Academy mean to shame and stigmatize her?
- Was it their goal to encourage other students to opt for abortion in the future?
- Did the Heritage school board intend to undermine their school and do its reputation damage by enforcing what they took to be the integrity of the honor code?

Of course, the answer to all of the above is "No."

The bitter irony—the bitter biblical irony—is that everyone involved was doing what they took to be the good.

Everyone involved was doing what they took to be the good.

But through them . . . .

Through them, a different outcome entirely was worked.

And the passive voice there reveals everything.

———

If the Apostle Paul's Letter to the Romans was a play instead of an epistle, if it was a script with a *Dramatis Personae* at the beginning, then it would be obvious even before you read it that in Romans, Sin has a starring role.

Now, I know, if you all wanted to hear about sin, you wouldn't have fled your Baptist and Catholic upbringings for a denomination where our only strong conviction is that "God is nice."

You all don't want to hear about sin; *no one* wants to hear about sin anymore.

But the drama of Paul's Gospel story of rectification by grace is unintelligible without Sin as a primary cast member. Paul's plot is incomplete without Sin as a main character.

Don't buy it?

In all of his letters, Paul uses the word sin (*hamartia*) 81 times, more than he uses any other word. Of those 81 times, 60 occur in his Letter to the Romans.

Over two-thirds of those usages occur right here in this chunk of Romans, chapters 5 through 8.

I realize you don't want to hear about sin in church, but you need to realize the sin you don't want to hear about in church is not sin as Paul most often uses the word in Romans.

Sin, for Paul, is not primarily a behavior.

Sin is not something we do.

Sin is not premarital sex, out-of-wedlock pregnancy, or self-righteously slut-shaming a teenage girl.

Sin is not something we do; Sin is a Something that Does.

Sin is not a lowercase transgression.

Sin is an uppercase Power.

A Power that ensnares and enslaves and stands over and against God.

Sin is a Power whose ultimate defeat the cross and resurrection portend.

Sin is an Agency—a Power synonymous with the Power of Satan.

It's Sin with a capital S.

Just notice how Paul here in Romans 7 doesn't use Sin as the verb we do but as the subjects of its own verbs: *"…it is no longer I that do it, but Sin that dwells within me."*

And again in verse 20: "…if I do what I do not want, it is no longer I that do it but Sin that dwells within me…"

Literally, in the Greek, it's: "…if I do what I do not want, it is no longer I that do it but Sin that has set up a base of operations within me."

It's a military term. Just as he has in the preceding chapters, the language Paul uses here in Romans 7 is the language of battle and war.

Sin isn't an attribute of us; Sin is an Antagonist against us.

Sin isn't a character flaw in you—that's the sin no one wants to hear about in church.

Sin isn't a character flaw in you.

Sin is cosmic terrorist that can invade even you.

Sin is an Enemy that can set up a base of operations within you.

———

Notice what Paul doesn't say in Romans 7.

Notice that Paul doesn't say he is *unable* to do the good that he wants to do.

Paul doesn't say he is *incapable* of willing the good he wishes to accomplish.

The problem isn't that he's *impotent* to will the good. The problem is not that he knows the good in his head but he can't bring his heart or his hands to choose it.

No, that's not it.

The problem isn't that he's impotent.

The problem is that he is not.

He wills the good that he wants to do—he is able.

He does the good he wants to do, but, in doing the good, what he produces, what his good act accomplishes is unrecognizable to his intention.

No good deed goes unpunished, we say.

But what Paul is saying: every good deed turns out as a kind of punishment. Every good deed ends up destructive.

"I can will what is right, but I cannot accomplish it. For I do not end up doing the good I want but the evil I do not want is what I accomplish."

Don't let the switch to the first-person singular in chapter 7 fool you.

Paul hasn't changed the subject.

Paul's not describing his inner conflict; Paul's describing an invasion.

His problem isn't a divided self but a self enslaved to Another. As he says plainly in verse 14, he's talking about the Self bound to a Slave Master.

Paul's not narrating shock at seeing what he has done despite his best intentions. He's narrating the shock at seeing what Sin has done through him, disguised in his best intentions.

William Faulkner said the theme of all lasting literature is the human heart in conflict with itself. Faulkner may be right about literature, but Paul is not writing fiction.

Paul isn't writing here about the human heart in conflict with itself.

Paul doesn't mean that there is an alter-ego within each us, contending against us.

No, Paul means that there is an Antagonist at work in the world, contending against God, an Alien Power that can reach as far down as into us and twist even our good works to evil.

We can will Life, Paul says, but through us Sin can will Death.

And not just through us- Paul says the contagion of Sin's reach extends even into God's own Law:

"The Law is holy and just and good. But Sin, seizing an opportunity in the Law, deceived me and through the Law killed me."

You see, this is why Paul argues so aggressively against requiring Gentile converts to obey the Jewish Law. It's why he's so adamant that requiring Gentile converts to follow the Law is in fact a false Gospel.

It's not because the Law in and of itself is bad or evil. And it's not simply that Paul wants to lower the bar for admission because adult circumcision is a tough sell.

It's that the Law has been taken hostage by the Power of Sin such that the faithful religious person in their service to God actually serves the Lordship of Sin.

That's the awful mystery with which Paul wrestles here in Romans 7.

It's not the mystery of the human heart in conflict with itself.

It's the mystery of God's Law and God's People twisted, unwittingly, into conflict against God.

It's the horror that the Power of Sin can co-opt and contravene even the religion God gave us, so that the outcome of our faithful actions ends up in contradiction to their intent.

The awful mystery with which Paul wrestles here is that even in serving God the religious person can in fact be serving God's Enemy.

And if you need an example of what Paul has in mind by this awful mystery, Exhibit A is hanging on the altar wall.

Look at that and listen to Paul again:

"I can will what is right, but I cannot accomplish it. For I do not end up doing the good I want but the evil I do not want is what I produce."

Evil is not its own agency.

Evil is what the Power of Sin does through the minions it fools and conscripts as accomplices. Through the Law, through Religion, through People of Piety.

For six chapters, the Apostle Paul has been narrating Sin's long resume. He's called it a Power. He's called it a King. He's called it a Wage-Master and a Slaver-Taker. He's given it adjectives like Dominion and Lordship. He's given it synonyms like Death and Satan.

But on Sin's resume, Paul saves this talk of the Law and the Enslaved Self for last.

Paul saves the worst for last.

He saves the Law and the enslaved "I" for last because for Paul there is no more awful accomplishment of Sin, no grosser testament to the demonic Power of Sin than Sin's ability to pervert even the best of our piety, to make a wretch of the most sincere religious person, to take even our godly obedience- even our *obedience*- and twist it to ungodly ends.

Paul saves the worst for last.

The Power of Sin is so insidious that the biggest threat to your soul...is you.

———

Show of hands—

Heritage Academy's Principal, David Hobbs—how many of you think that he heard about Maddi Runkles's pregnancy and said to himself "I think I'm going to shame and stigmatize a student today."

Do you think Principal David Hobbs woke up one morning and said to himself "I think I'd like to drag my school's reputation through the mud, make its leaders look like hypocrites, and make our religion look ridiculous and shallow."

Do you think he and his school board members put their heads together and chose to be the bad guys in the story?

If your reaction to this newspaper story is to villainize the principal and the school board members as stigmatizing, self-righteous, slut-shaming sexists, if your immediate impulse is to judge them, then you're not hearing the Apostle Paul today.

It's only in comic books that villains choose to be villains. And only in comic books do the villains know they are villains from the get-go.

The rest of us, St. Paul says, set out to serve the Good, to serve God, and only later discover ourselves to be serving his Enemy.

By all accounts Principal David Hobbs is a much experienced and much more beloved educator.

He and the school board reached their decision to discipline Maddi only after "much prayer and scripture-study and spiritual discernment."

In an interview, Principal Hobbs said: "We do believe in forgiveness, but forgiveness does not mean there is no accountability."

And guess what?

He's right.

Forgiveness is not the opposite of accountability; in fact, forgiveness without accountability is what the Church calls cheap grace.

In that same interview, Principal Hobbs explained: "We teach our students about the beauty of marriage and that sex inside marriage is what Christians believe God desires for marriage and is one of the attributes that makes it beautiful."

Again, he's right. That is what the Church teaches, what all Christian traditions teach.

The good that David Hobbs and the Heritage Academy school board pursued *is* a godly good.

And yet—and yet … through them…

As Kristen Hawkins, President of Students for Life, said to the *Washington Post*:

"What this school is doing in advocating for Christian morality is the antithesis of being Christian."

What they've done is the antithesis of what they sought to do.

Or, as the Apostle Paul puts it: "Sin, seizing an opportunity in Religion, deceived them and through them…"

Maddi Runkles and Heritage Academy Christian School—that's just one small story ripped from the newspaper.

Never mind what Karl Barth said, you don't need the *New York Times*.

Just think about your own daily domestic destruction—we do the most damage to the people we love most and, most often, the damage we do we do in trying to do them good.

Or rather, *we* don't do them damage.

But through us…through us…

The Power that has set up a base of operations within us … can pervert even our best and most faithful and loving intentions.

———

Christians like Principal David Hobbs, Christians like the school board members at Heritage Academy, Christians like Maddi Runkles's slut-shaming friends—they're all the kinds of Christians who make Non-Christians write off Christianity.

Let's face it—

That's how Maddi's story made it into outlets like the *New York Times*; it's a salacious story that undermines Christianity in the public eye.

But frankly, I'm sick and tired of people who try to dismiss Christianity because every Sunday Christians like you are just as petty and racist and passive-aggressive and sexist and corrupt and apathetic and hypocritical and greedy as everyone else.

Really, Christians like Principal David Hobbs and the Heritage Academy school board members and the straight-A, born-again slut-shamers—imperfect and immoral and hypocritical Christians like you—they're not an argument *against* Christianity; they're the best argument *for* Christianity.

Because if St. Paul is right, if the Power of Sin is so insidious it can pervert even the best of our piety, twist our most godly acts to ungodly ends, then that means absolutely NO ONE can claim that they do not need Jesus Christ.

If the Power of Sin is such that it can turn God's saints into unwitting servants of God's Enemy, if even the best of us cannot be good, then nothing you do can be relied upon to make you right with

God, to rectify the balance sheet of your life, to justify you before the judgement of God.

If Paul is right about the Power of Sin, then nothing you do — not your piety or your prayers, not your religion or your resume, not your good deeds or your good name, not your charity or your character or your career or your church attendance, not your beliefs or your bible study — nothing you do can be relied upon to justify you before God because in all of it, Paul says, you could just as likely be serving God's Enemy.

If Paul is right, if the Power of Sin is such that it can pervert what we do for God for the Enemy's own ends, then we can never trust what we have done.

We can never trust what we have done *to justify us*.

We can only ever trust what God has done for us.

————

Imperfect, impatient, petty, immoral, hypocritical Christians — you're the best argument *for* Christianity because if the Power of Sin is such that it can corrupt even you then NO ONE, absolutely NO ONE, NOBODY can say that they do not need the justification that God offers us by grace alone in Jesus Christ.

No one —

No one here

And no one who would never be caught dead in here

No one

Religious or Irreligious

Secular or Spiritual

Christian or Non-Christian

Sinner or Supposed Saint

No one can say they do not need Jesus Christ.

Because no one can say for sure that in serving God they haven't actually been serving Another instead.

The fact is — you don't need to believe Paul.

The truth of it is all over the newspaper every day.

We can never be certain which Lord we're really serving.

Which makes you — me — the perfect argument not against the Gospel but for it. Because the Gospel message is that no matter what you have done, because of what Christ has done, regardless of what Lord you have served, our Lord declares you in the right. As a gift.

That's good news.

Romans 8:12-17 - Long Live The Revolution!

Taylor Mertins

So then, brothers and sisters, we are debtors, not to the flesh, to live according to the flesh – for if you live according to the flesh, you will die; but if by the Spirit you put to death the deeds of the body, you will live. For all who are led by the Spirit of God are children of God. For you did not receive a spirit of slavery to fall back into fear, but you have received a spirit of adoption. When we cry, 'Abba! Father!' it is that very Spirit bearing witness with our spirit that we are children of God, and if children, then heirs, heirs of God and joint heirs with Christ – if, in fact, we suffer with him so that we may also be glorified with him. For all who are led by the Spirit of God are children of God, and if children, then heirs, heirs of God and joint heirs with Christ.

- Romans 8.12-17

I love going home to visit family. There is just something special about visiting the old haunts and showing off a baby to make me really nostalgic for the past. Last week Lindsey and I spent some time up in Alexandria with my family, and it felt like nothing, and everything, had changed. For instance: When I went to the grocery store I bumped into a couple people I used to go to church with, but then when I drove out on Route 1 all the old buildings were gone and were replaced with town homes. **Time, like a river, moves and though it looks the same, everything changes.**

But perhaps the thing I enjoy most about going home is spending time with my grandmothers; **Gran and Omi**, both of whom are now great-grandmothers to Elijah. I know I'm biased, but I do have the best grandmothers in the world. One represents all the good southern hospitality that Petersburg, VA has ever had to offer and the other represents the refined qualities of old Europe with her charm and presence. They could not be more different from one another, and yet they are incredibly close.

Anyway, whenever I head home, whether it's for a day or a week, I always plan on swinging by both of their homes unannounced. And last week was no exception.

Both visits were similar – we had the usual chit chat, we caught up on all the other family members, we shared stories about Staunton, and then we watched Elijah crawl all over the place. During our time together we learned about different health concerns, new aches and pains, and were unable to confront the reality that one day, perhaps not for some time, but nevertheless one day, they will no longer be here.

Each visit ended with both of them asking us to stay longer, while Elijah fussed for food or for a nap. And both visits ended with the exact same words from both of my grandmothers: **"I just wish I had something to give you."** To which one looked around the room as if to give us something off the coffee table, and the other went upstairs and literally took a painting off the wall and put it in our hands.

I just wish I had something to give you.

"When we cry, 'Abba! Father!' it is that very Spirit bearing witness with our spirit that we are children of God, and if children, then heirs, heirs of God and joint heirs with Christ."

Inheritance, being an heir, is always a complex matter. I wish it wasn't true, but I've helped families prepare for funerals when more of the conversation around the table was focused on who was receiving what than what hymns or scripture would their now dead loved one want in their Service of Death and Resurrection. At the moment when a family needs to be together almost more than ever, they were already marking the territory of their hopeful inheritance.

Most of the time, we can't choose what we inherit. Our parents or grandparents might think something has special significance for us, and therefore leave that item for us in the will, but rare are the times that we get to declare what we shall receive.

And there are others things that we have no choice about inheriting. We get the good and the bad, the responsibility and the privilege, the shame and the pride.

Frankly, three of things that determine our lives more than anything else come to us without a choice at all: **We do not choose the family we are born into, we do not choose the color of our skin, and we do not choose the economic status of our families.** We inherit all three without any action of our own, and those three things set us on a trajectory that we can rarely alter.

And of course there are things we inherit through the sands of time that we'd rather erase; like the celebrities who get their DNA tested for television shows about genealogy only to discover that their ancestors were part of the Nazi regime, or were slave owners, or participated in the near-eradication of the indigenous peoples in this country.

Inheritance is a complicated and confusing thing. **Are we nothing more than the genes and the history we inherit? Can we break from the tyranny of expectation and what it means to be an heir? Who are we really?**

St. Paul says that we are children and heirs of God!

Our inheritance, unlike that which we receive from our families, is totally different from anything that has ever existed. Moths and rust do not corrupt it; thieves cannot break in and steal it. It cannot be lost in the fall of the stock market, or burned in the night, or taken by the government in the so-called death tax.

Our inheritance is our hope while everything else appears to fail. It promises a future when we cannot imagine there being anything left for us in this life.

It is nothing short of the glory of the Lord.

However, and **this is a big however**, there is more to this inheritance than smiles and rainbows and resurrection. It comforts AND it afflicts.

We receive something so remarkable and inexplicable as heirs with Christ, but it also comes with a cost. Receiving this gift puts at risk our financial security, our reputation, our social position, our friends, our family, our everything.

This is the revolution of faith.

We are fellow heirs with Jesus Christ, we shall receive resurrection, but we also suffer with the Lord.

The time is coming, and is indeed here, when the mighty will be brought low and the lowly will be raised high. Seek ye first the kingdom of God and do not put your trust in things that will fade away with the blowing of the wind. You need only faith the size of a mustard seed. Ask you shall receive. Those who lose their lives for the sake of the gospel will live.

Have you ever heard anything more revolutionary in your lives?

Everything about our existence changes with the inheritance of the Lord: Our finances change when we realize that all we receive first comes from the Lord. Our families change when we realize that all who do the will of God are our mothers, fathers, brothers, and sisters. Our worldviews change when we realize that God is contending against the powers and principalities here and now.

All that we held so near and dear before will wash away when the tide of life comes in. Moths will eat away at the fabric of our perspectives, thieves will steal the wealth that we think determines everything, but there is one thing that endures forever: **Jesus Christ.**

This is nothing short of revolutionary. And to be honest, it's gotten a lot of people killed throughout the centuries, including the One in whom we lie and move.

That's one of the things we struggle to remember, here in our comfortable Christianity; Jesus was a revolutionary. He was not killed for loving too much. He was killed for calling into question who was really in charge, for confronting the elite about not taking care of the poor and the marginalized, and for telling the truth.

Jesus was a revolutionary and calls us to join the revolution. But here in Staunton, we don't feel very revolutionary.

We like what we have: good schools, perfectly manicured lawns, children that come home to visit, vacations, golf courses, solid retirement portfolios. We can't imagine being called to leave our families, or go to prison, or even lose our lives for the sake of the gospel. Why do we need to risk anything when we already have everything we want?

We, the people who have this remarkable inheritance through the Lord, can take all kinds of risks that the rest of the world fears. We know where all of our gifts really come from and that we can give them away, we know that our time is a fleeting and precious thing that we can give away, we know that even our lives are worth giving away because they were first given to us.

We can, and should, be reckless with our lives because we can afford to be. We've been given the greatest inheritance in the history of the world. Why aren't we doing anything with it?

There was an uncle who had amassed a great fortune throughout his life, he started his own business and invested wisely, but had no children to leave his wealth to. However, he did have a couple nieces and nephews who patiently waited with baited breath for him to die so they could reap the benefits of the inheritance. While they should have been committing themselves to their educations and their careers, they just daydreamed about what they would do with the money as soon as their uncle died.

And then he did.

The siblings all met with the family lawyer after the funeral, trying their best to appear mournful while hiding smiles of utmost glee. The lawyer took his time reading through the important legal jargon until he came to the inheritance: To my nieces and nephews I leave... they gripped the leather chairs with anticipation... my library.

"Library?" they all thought silently though one of them accidentally shouted it out loud. "What about our money?!?!"

They all left in a storm of rage angered beyond belief, but the youngest nephew waited behind, and he signed for the inheritance library, and gave the lawyer the address of his house.

For days he unpacked box after box of books and started stacking them wherever he could. It began feeling like the books were becoming the new wallpaper, and for years they just sat their collecting dust. And the longer they remained, the more the man resented the books.

His life continued on, he got married, had a few kids, got divorced, lost the job, and started spending all his time at home. As he aged he felt like the books were there to taunt him, mocking him from every corner. And then one day, it a fit of built-up rage, he ran to the nearest stack, grabbed the top-most book and threw it across the room.

WHAM! The hardback left a perfect rectangular indentation in the wall from the force of the throw while the aging man breathed heavily with his hands clenched tightly together. He then slowly walked over to the wall to pick up the remaining remnants of the book to throw them away when he noticed something strange on the floor: a couple $100 bills.

It only took a moment, the slightest measure of time, before he realized what he had just discovered. The missing fortune of his uncle was in the library of books, hidden in between the covers, hundreds of thousands of dollars.

When we cry, 'Abba! Father!' it is that very Spirit bearing witness with our spirit that we are children of God, and if children, then heirs, heirs of God and joint heirs with Christ – if, in fact, we suffer with him so that we may also be glorified with him.

We are joint heirs with Christ, and have received an everlasting inheritance that is our present and future glory! Are we letting this inheritance gather dust on the bookshelves of our lives? Do we know what we've received?!

God is bold and generous with reckless abandon to the point of giving his only begotten Son so that we might have eternal life. God is concerned with the cries of the needy and plight of the marginalized. God brings down the mighty and raises the lowly.

And so should we.

Long live the revolution! Amen.

Romans 8:31-39 - Sinners in the Hands of a _____ God

Jason Micheli

What then are we to say about these things? If God is for us, who is against us? He who did not withhold his own Son, but gave him up for all of us, will he not with him also give us everything else? Who will bring any charge against God's elect? It is God who justifies. Who is to condemn? It is Christ Jesus, who died, yes, who was raised, who is at the right hand of God, who indeed intercedes for us. Who will separate us from the love of Christ? Will hardship, or distress, or persecution, or famine, or nakedness, or peril, or sword? As it is written, "For your sake we are being killed all day long; we are accounted as sheep to be slaughtered." No, in all these things we are more than conquerors through him who loved us. For I am convinced that neither death, nor life, nor angels, nor rulers, nor things present, nor things to come, nor powers, nor height, nor depth, nor anything else in all creation, will be able to separate us from the love of God in Christ Jesus our Lord.

—Romans 8:31-39

Who is against us? Who will condemn us?

Who can separate us from the love of Christ?

For the Apostle Paul, these are rhetorical questions.

They're Paul's way of implying that if you sense any ambiguity about the answer, if you feel any uncertainty about the conclusion, then you should go back to chapter 1, verse 1 and start over.

Reread his letter to the Romans-because Paul's left you no room for qualification. There's no grist for doubt or debate or indecision.

Don't left the punctuation marks fool you because there's only one possible way to answer the questions Paul's laid out for you.

No one.

No one is against us.

No one will condemn us.

No one, no thing, nothing can separate us from Christ's love.

Of course, as a preacher, I know first-hand the danger in asking rhetorical questions is that there's always one or two listeners in the audience who don't realize that the question you're asking has no answer but the obvious one.

The danger in asking rhetorical questions is that there's always one or two people who mistakenly think the question might have a different answer.

For example, take this response to Paul's rhetorical questions from Mark Driscoll:

[*Play clip from "God Hates You": "Some of you, God hates you. Some of you, God is sick of you. God is frustrated with you. God is wearied by you. God has suffered long enough with you. He doesn't think you're cute. He doesn't think it's funny. He doesn't think your excuse is meritorious. He doesn't care if you compare yourself to someone worse than you, He hates them too. God hates, right now, personally, objectively hates some of you."*]

I thought that would get your attention.

Or at least make you grateful I'm your pastor.

Just think, I make a single joke on my blog about Jesus farting and some of you write letters to the bishop; Mark Driscoll preaches an entire sermon about how "God hates you" and thousands of people like it on Facebook.

If you read my blog, then you know I feel about Mark Driscoll the same way I feel about Joel Osteen, Testicular Cancer, and Verizon Wireless.

But he's not an obscure, street-corner, fire-and-brimstone preacher.

He's a best-selling author. He's planted churches all over the world.

The church he founded in Seattle, Mars Hill, is one of the nation's largest churches with a membership that is younger and more diverse than almost any other congregation.

Ten thousand listened to that sermon that Sunday.

And that Sunday ten thousand did NOT get up and walk out.

That Sunday ten thousand listened to the proclamation that "God hates you, God hates the you you really are, the person you are at your deepest level."

And that Sunday at the end of that sermon somewhere near ten thousand people said "Amen."

Which, of course, means "That's true."

Except it isn't.

Maybe I shouldn't be surprised.

After all, technically speaking, it's a 'good' sermon. It's visceral. It's urgent. It's confrontational and convicting.

It's the kind of preaching that demands a response.

Technically speaking, I bet the sermon "worked."

I bet it scared the hell out of people.

But what did it scare them into I wonder?

Because when it comes to Paul's rhetorical questions, Mark Driscoll gets the response dead wrong. So dead wrong that anti-Christ is probably the most accurate term to describe it.

He's wrong.

But you know that already.

I can tell from the grimace of disgust you had on your face while listening to him that you know that already.

You don't need to be a pastor to know he's wrong. And you don't need to be a pastor to *prove* he's wrong.

All you need are a handful of memory verses.

Memory verses like Colossians 1.15: "Jesus Christ is the exact image of the invisible God."

Which means: God is like Jesus.

And God doesn't change.

Which means: God has always been like Jesus and God will always be like Jesus.

So no, God doesn't hate you. God has never hated you and God would never hate you.

You don't need to be pastor to prove he's wrong; you just need to remember that John 3.16 does not say *"God so loathed the world that he took Jesus' life instead of yours."*

No, it says "God so loved ... that he gave ..."

You don't need to be a pastor to know that God isn't fed up with you. God isn't sick and tired of you. God doesn't hate the you in you because *"God was in Christ reconciling all things—all things—to himself."*

In case you forgot, that's 2 Corinthians 5.19.

It's true that God is just and God is holy and anyone who reads the newspaper has got to think God's entitled to a little anger, but you don't have to be a pastor to know that none of those attributes trump the Paul's Gospel summation that *"while we were still sinners, God died for the ungodly, for us."*

God has not had it up to anywhere with you.

You don't need to have gone to seminary to know that; you just need to have gone to church on June 30.

That's when we heard Paul testify from his personal experience that no matter how much we sin, no matter how often we sin, no matter how we sin, no matter how much our *sin abounds, God's grace abounds all the more.*

So that—

'There is therefore now no condemnation..."

"We have peace with God..."

Whatever needed to be set right, whatever needed to be forgiven, whatever needed to be paid, *"it is finished."* That's in red letters in my bible. Jesus said it.

His cross, the Letter to the Hebrews says, was **"a perfect sacrifice, once for all."**

For all.

So there's nothing in your present, there's nothing in your past, there's nothing coming down the pike—and just in case you think you're the exception let's just say *there's nothing in all of creation—* there's nothing that can separate you from the love of God.

You don't have to be a pastor to realize that you can say this a whole lot of different ways, but it all boils down to the same simple message:

God is for us.

Not against us.

But you know that.

Mark Driscoll may have 10,000 people in his church but I'd bet every last one of you would run him out of this church.

You would never sit through a sermon like. You would never tolerate a preacher like that—you barely tolerate me.

You would never participate in a church that had perverted the Gospel into that.

God hates you. God's fed up with you. God's sick and tired of you. God's suffered long enough with you.

God's against you.

You would NEVER say that to someone else. Ever.

But here's the thing — and maybe you do need to be a pastor know this:

There are plenty of you
who say things like that
to yourselves
all the time.

Not one of you would ever say things like that to someone else, but, consider it on the job knowledge, plenty of you say it to yourself every day.

Plenty of you "know" Paul's questions are rhetorical.

You know there's only one possible answer, only one way to respond: God is for us.

And yet...

When it comes to you and your life and what you've done and how God must feel about the person you see in the mirror, your inner monologue sounds a whole lot more like Mark Driscoll than it sounds like Paul.

You may not know this, but as a pastor I definitely do.

Even though you'd never say it in a sermon, you tell yourself that surely God's fed up with you for the mess you made of your marriage or the mistakes you made with your kids or the ways your life hasn't measured up.

Even though you'd never dream of saying to someone else "there's no way God will forgive that." that's exactly what you tell yourself when it comes to the secret that God knows but your spouse doesn't.

Even though there's no way you'd ever consider saying it to someone else, you still tell yourself that there's no way your faith is deep enough, commitment strong enough, beliefs firm enough to ever please God.

Even though it would never cross your mind to say to someone else "God must be angry with you for something ... God must be punishing you ..." many of you can't get that out of your mind when you receive a diagnosis or suffer the death of someone close to you.

God hates you. God's fed up with you. God's sick and tired of you. God's suffered long enough with you.

I can't think of one of you who would let a voice like Mark Driscoll's into this pulpit on a Sunday morning.

And yet I can think of a whole lot of us who every day let a voice just like his into our heads.

———

So here's my question: why?

I mean—we know Paul's being rhetorical. We know it's obvious. We know there's only one possible response: God is for us.

So why?

Why do we persist in imagining that God is angry or impatient or wearied or judgmental or vindictive or ungracious or unforgiving?

If it's obvious enough for a rhetorical question, then why?

Why do we persist in imagining that God is like anything other than Jesus?

Is it because we tripped up on those bible verses that speak of God's anger?

Maybe.

Is it because we've all heard preachers or we all know Christians who sound a little like Mark Driscoll?

Sure we have.

Is it because we're convinced the sin in our lives is so great, so serious, that we're the exception to Paul's ironclad, Gospel equation: God is for us?

Is it because we think we're the exception?

Maybe for some of us.

But I wonder.

I wonder if we persist in imagining that God is angry and impatient and unforgiving and at the end of his rope—I wonder if we imagine God is like that because that's what we're like.

I wonder if we imagine God must be angry because we carry around so much anger with us?

I wonder if we imagine there are some things even God can't forgive because there are things we won't forgive?

I wonder if we imagine that God's at the end of his rope because there are plenty of people with whom we're at the end of ours?

———

I've been open with you in the past about my sometimes rocky, sometimes resuscitated relationship with my Dad.

I've told you about how my dad and me—we have a history that started when I was about the age my youngest boy is now.

And I've told you about how even today our relationship is tense and complicated ... sticky—the way it always is in a family when addiction and infidelity and abuse are part of a story that ends in separation.

As with any separation, all the relationships in the family got complicated. And as with many separations, what happens in childhood reverberates well into adulthood.

What I haven't told you before is that I had a falling out, over a year ago, with my Mom.

The kind of falling out where you can no longer remember what or who started it or if it was even important.

The kind of rift that seemed to pull down every successive conversation like an undertow.

The kind of argument that starts out in anger and then slowly advances on both sides towards a stubborn refusal to forgive and eventually ages into a sad resignation that this is what the relationship is now, that this is what it will be, that this thing is between us now and is going to stay there.

We had that falling out quite a while ago, and I've let it fester simply because I didn't have the energy to do the work I knew it would take to repair it.

And, to be honest, I didn't have the faith to believe it could be repaired.

There's no way I can say this without it sounding contrived and cliché.

There's no way I can say this without it sounding exactly like the sort of sentimental BS you might expect in a sermon.

So I'll just say it straight up and if it makes you want to vomit go ahead. I read Romans 8 late this week and it ... convicted me.

And so I called my Mom.

"We need to talk" I said.

"You really think so?"

I didn't know how to answer.

It was a rhetorical question. There was only one possible answer: yes.

And so I began by telling her that I'd been reading a part of the bible and that I'd just noticed something I'd never noticed before.

I don't know why I'd never noticed it before.

Romans 8:31-39 is, after all, one of the most popular scripture texts for funerals. I've preached on this scripture probably more than any other biblical text.

Yet preaching it for funerals, with death and eternity looming, I never noticed how this passage about how no one is against us, how no one will condemn us, how nothing can separate us from the love of God in Christ Jesus—it comes at the end of Paul's chapter on the Holy Spirit.

It comes as the conclusion to Paul talking about how we are to live according to the Spirit—according to Christ's Spirit.

It comes as the conclusion to Paul talking about how we are the heirs of Christ's ministry, about how that inheritance will involve certainly suffering but that the Spirit will help us in our weakness.

This "nothing shall separate us" passage—it comes as the conclusion to Paul telling us how the Holy Spirit will work in our lives to conform us to Christ's image so that we might live up to and in to calling.

In all the times I've turned to Romans 8 for a funeral sermon, I've never noticed before that, for Paul, it's not about eternity.

It's about living eternity now.

Who is against us? Who will condemn us?

Who can separate us from the love of Christ?

Paul's questions might be rhetorical.

The answers might be obvious and certain.

But that doesn't make them easy or simple.

I'd never noticed that for Paul here in Romans 8—it's actually meant to be the kind of preaching that demands a response.

Because if you believe that God in Jesus Christ is unconditionally, no matter what, *for us* then you've also got to believe that you should not hold anything against someone else.

If you believe that God in Christ Jesus refuses—gratuitously—to condemn your life, then you've got to at least believe that it should be ditto for the people in your life.

And if you believe that nothing can separate us from the love of God in Christ Jesus, nothing in all creation, then you must also believe that *because of the love of God in Christ Jesus* then nothing, nothing, nothing can separate us.

From one another.

Romans 8:21-39 - On Working The Crowd

Taylor Mertins

What then are we to say about these things? If God is for us, who is against us? He who did not withhold his own Son, but gave him up for all of us, will he not with him also give us everything else? Who will bring any charge against God's elect? It is God who justifies. Who is to condemn? It is Christ Jesus, who died, yes, who was raised, who is at the right hand of God, who indeed intercedes for us. Who will separate us from the love of Christ? Will hardship, or distress, or persecution, or famine, or nakedness, or peril, or sword? As it is written, 'For your sake we are being killed all day long; we are accounted as sheep to be slaughtered.' No, in all these things we are more than conquerors through him who loved us. For I am convinced that neither death, nor life, nor angels, nor rulers, nor things present, nor things to come, nor powers, nor height, nor depth, nor anything else in all creation, will be able to separate us from the love of God in Christ Jesus our Lord. For I am convinced that neither death, nor life, nor angels, nor rulers, nor things present, nor things to come, nor powers, not height, nor depth, nor anything else in all creation, will be able to separate us from the love of God in Christ Jesus our Lord.

- Romans 8.31-39

Working a crowd can be an art form. Comedians walk back and forth casually across a stage making the crowds feel relaxed and ready to laugh. Martin Luther King Jr. repeatedly punctuated and staccato'd his refrains like the rhythm of a song to get the people connected to the message. Even our President, Donald Trump, knew how to work the crowds at his rallies leading up to the election. You don't win elections by laying out the step-by-step plans to make economic, ethical, political, and militaristic changes. You don't win elections by calmly reflecting on the days of the past and a desire for simpler times. You don't win elections with PowerPoint projections of pie-graphs and political policies.

We all know you win elections by firing up the people with a litany of complaints about what has gone wrong. You win elections by throwing gasoline onto the fire. You win elections by working the crowd.

And Jesus, like Donald Trump, knew how to work a crowd.

You spread the word and get thousands of people outside to hear the message, you keep them on the edge of their, you know, ground area, and then wait for them to salivate with under the sun and then transform a loaf of bread and a couple of fish into a buffet the likes of which had never been seen.

You get the crowds riled up about working on the Sabbath, even quote some of the prophets from the past, and then heal a cripple man and leave everyone with a rhetorical question: Is it better to heal someone on the Sabbath or let them continue to suffer?

Walk into the middle of an angry mob about to stone a woman to death and quietly write a couple choice words in the sand to let them peer deeply into their own sinful souls and then empower the woman to live a new life.

Jesus knew how to work the crowd.

And Palm Sunday, this strange occasion where we pass out palm branches at the beginning of the service, is perhaps the best example of Jesus' perfect political ability to work the crowd. We read that many people spread their cloaks; they literally take the clothes off their backs, and placed them on the road. And still yet others even cut down palm branches to prepare the way for the king who entered Jerusalem on the back of a donkey.

We know the story. We can imagine ourselves there on the side of the road with the dust hanging in the air. We can feel the buzz of expectation around the one who will come to change it all. We can feel within ourselves that same desire to scream out **"Hosanna!" "Save us!"**

But, unlike the crowd, we know how the story ends.

We know what awaits us this so-called Holy Week. **We know** what will happen in the temple when Jesus flips the tables. **We know** what kind of strange sermon Jesus will offer from the mountain. **We know** that Jesus will get down on the floor and wash the feet of his disciples. **We know** that Jesus will gather his friends around a table to

110

share bread and wine. **We know** that Jesus will be betrayed, arrested, beaten, mocked, and nailed to a cross. **We know** that before the end of the week, Jesus will die.

And because we know how the story ends, it becomes clear to us that may not have known what we were doing by joining the crowds along the road, or by joining the crowds in a place like this one that we call church.

The crowds who gathered to sing their "hosannas" wanted a king, but the only people who continue to admire him as a king at the end of the week are the sadistic soldiers who made him a crown of thorns and drove it into his skin.

Jesus, it seems, was not the right kind of king. He was not the one they, or even we, were hoping for.

Maybe Jesus wasn't all that gifted at working the crowd. After all, it took less than a week for the shouts to go from "Hosanna" to "crucify."

Jesus is a King unlike any other king. Other kings, who are also at times called presidents, know they have to work and manipulate the crowd to bend them according to the desires of the powerful. Kings and Presidents may even rely on the power of the sword to control and handle the crowd to bring forth their hopes and dreams.

Such is the reality of worldly power.

But Jesus, our King, does not take advantage of the crowd's enthusiasm. Rather than a call to arms to storm the city gates or to murder the ruling elite, Jesus suffers humiliation, abandonment, and death.

Do you still want to be part of the crowd by the side of the road? Do you want a place in Jesus' kingdom? Do you want to follow the suffering King?

Don't be mistaken; Jesus is as political as they come. But he rules not at the head of an army, but from an old wooden cross. He rules not by filibustering particular Supreme Court nominees or demanding democratic political policies, but by laying it all down for the ungodly. He rules not by ordering his troops to use chemical weapons against innocent civilians or even sending tomahawk missiles to destroy a military base, but mounting the cross and saying, "Forgive them Father, for they do not know what they are doing."

In America, we pride ourselves on being the ones who can defy the whims of the crowds. Freedom! We think for ourselves! **Or at least, we think we can think for ourselves.** But here's the irony: The moment we are so sure that we have thought something up for ourselves, the moment we believe we are most free, is really when we've been co-opted by the powerful.

I know that we like to think that if we had been there, we would've been good disciples and that we would've stayed with Jesus to the very end. I know we like to think that if we had been there in Germany all those years ago, that we would've protected the Jews and rallied against Hitler. I know we like to think that if we had been involved in politics at the time, we would've voted against going to war in Iraq and Afghanistan.

But the truth is a whole lot harder to swallow: We are easily manipulated.

Which is precisely why we sing awful songs like "Ah Holy Jesus." God will not allow us to get away with perennial self-deception and arrogance. We killed Jesus.

Who was the guilty? Who brought this upon thee? Alas, my treason, Jesus, hath undone thee! 'Twas I, Lord Jesus, I it was denied thee; I crucified thee.

We know who we want Jesus to be. We want Jesus on our side in our petty arguments with friends and neighbors. We want Jesus on our side when it comes to disagreements in the community. We want Jesus on our side when it comes to the trajectory of our country. We want Jesus on our side when it comes to politics, and Syria, and Healthcare, and Immigration. We see ourselves as Jesus in the story of his entry into Jerusalem, when in reality we are far more like the fickle crowds on the side of the road than anyone else.

And that brings us to Romans 8.

Romans 8 is an unsettling text. Sure, we've heard it and used it at funerals; it offers us comfort and hope in the midst of sorrow and loss. It is important for us to declare over and over again that death will not separate us from the love of God in Christ Jesus.

We know this passage. We know it just like we know the story of Palm Sunday. In fact, if you can remember, months ago I asked the congregation to imagine what scripture you would use to comfort someone on death row, and this was the overwhelming favorite.

But these words from Paul can tempt us to forget that it is not just death that threatens to separate us from the love of God. Instead, we imagine the other things in the list to be good: life, angels, rulers, powers, things present, things to come. **But all of them can threaten to come between Christ and his church; between God and us.**

When we are comfortable, when we can't imagine our faith requiring us to suffer, the list remains easily ignorable. However, we become true disciples of Jesus when we are willing to take risks, when we are prepared to go against the flow, when we resist the manipulation of those in power. And risks are called risks for a reason: following Jesus is a risky thing to do because it always involves the possibility of rejection.

Many of us know that this week marked the anniversary of the death of Martin Luther King Jr. Dr. King stood firm while the waves of the status quo crashed around him. Dr. King called out the principalities and powers for being wrong. Dr. King worked the crowds to a belief in non-violent resistance. And it got him killed.

Here in Staunton, like I said last week, we don't feel very revolutionary, we don't equate our faith with taking risks, and we can't even imagine having to lay down our lives for the sake of the gospel. We can't imagine ourselves being like Dr. King or questioning what our country is doing in Syria. But if we are serious about following Jesus, we will suffer; it's just a less glamorous and more mundane form of suffering.

You know, like being mindful of other people; not getting stuck in our own unending bubble; asking hard questions that other people would rather ignore; acting like Jesus; sacrificing our wants and needs; calling someone in the midst of grief; showing up for a funeral when we might have other things to do.

Following Jesus in this place these days might not get us killed. But it might mean reaching out to someone who is totally unlike us. It might mean having a conversation with someone who voted for the other candidate. It might mean asking our spouses to forgive us for what we did. It might mean repenting for the way we spoke to our children or our parents. It might mean confronting our friends about their addictions. It might mean asking for help regarding our addictions.

And in so doing, we will suffer.

But nevertheless (!) nothing can separate us from the love of God in Jesus Christ! Not a bitter parent who refuses our apology; not an angry child who resents us for a past decision; not a nation who indiscriminately persecutes the poor and the marginalized; not a king or a president or a politician; not standing against the powers that be; not going against the current for a strange and more loving way of life; not anything now; not anything in the future.

We will surely suffer for the sake of the kingdom, but we will never be divided from the Lord. Amen

Romans 10:9-17 - Words are Always Necessary

Teer Hardy

"If you confess with your lips that Jesus is Lord and believe in your heart that God raised him from the dead, you will be saved. For one believes with the heart and so is justified, and one confesses with the mouth and so is saved. The scripture says, 'No one who believes in him will be put to shame.' For there is no distinction between Jew and Greek; the same Lord is Lord of all and is generous to all who call on him. For, 'Everyone who calls on the name of the Lord shall be saved.' But how are they to call on one in whom they have not believed? And how are they to believe in one of whom they have never heard? And how are they to hear without someone to proclaim him? And how are they to proclaim him unless they are sent? As it is written, 'How beautiful are the feet of those who bring good news!' But not all have obeyed the good news; for Isaiah says, 'Lord, who has believed our message?' So faith comes from what is heard, and what is heard comes through the word of Christ.

- Romans 10.9-17

I starred at the blank pages of paper in my Moleskin notebook for the better part of a day this week. I sat down to write praying, "Come on God, give me something good." When nothing came, I got up and found something else that need to be done. Later, I would sit back down at my desk, open my notebook, grab my favorite pen, and ask God again to give me something to say to you this morning.

One of the reasons I think I starred at blank pages of paper for so long this week is because I loved the saying, "Preach the Gospel and when necessary use words." As someone who until a year ago next week preached once a year it was a way for me to deal with the lack of space in the pulpit for me. The saying, "Preach the Gospel and when necessary use words," also lended itself to my passion for missions. Why use words when I could just use my hands and feet. After all, rebuilding a home or digging an irrigation trench in the Highlands of Guatemala seems easier than reading Karl Barth's *Church Dogmatics* or sitting through Systematic Theology with Kendall Soulen.

During Advent of 2012 Allison and I, along with a mission team from the church where I served as youth director, headed to the Highlands of Guatemala. There we literally did not use words to preach the Gospel because it would have needed to be translated twice in order for the Mayans we were serving to understand what we were saying. If you think a sermon is bad the first time through, imagine having the listen to it over and over again. While in the Highlands we worked as day-laborers while the money our church raised was used to employ local masons and plumbers. After the work day had ended we would head back to our host homes and share a meal together. Later in the evening we would do a Bible study together and the share communion with one another. Anyone who has been on a mission trip can tell you that when you preach the Gospel and do not use words there is an unbelievable spiritual high you experience. In the Highlands of Guatemala in December 2012 that mission trip high was even stronger because every night we shared communion with one another, I heard the Lord's Prayer in at least three different languages at the same time. It was as though we had our own Pentecost experience on a cold hill side in one of those places teachers tell our kids no longer exists.

But over the past few years (really since November 2016), especially in the last 51 weeks, I am convinced that we, all of us, need to rethink this Christian cliché. Not because mission work is bad or that we should not do it. But because on the surface it sounds great, "Preach the Gospel and when necessary use words," but once we dig deeper into the popular saying, it becomes problematic.

At it's most basic level, "Preach the Gospel and when necessary use words," means we as Christians talk too much about the Gospel instead of living it out. But from my lack of conversations with some of you about the Gospel, and the krpyonite powers my Bible seems to have with I place it on the table at Starbucks, I do not think this is the problem.

Paul's letter to the Romans is the most influential book of the Christian Bible for the ways that Paul's' words have influenced Christian doctrine and theology over the past 2000 years. Throughout his letter to the

Romans Paul is engaging the Hebrew scriptures making the case that the resurrected and ascended Jesus is in fact the Messiah, the One sent by God, and that now Jews and Gentiles are both invited into the new life made possible by the grace of God. This was an easier sell to the Gentiles, who had been previously outside the Abrahamic covenant, which is why Paul opens this chapter of Romans by making his case to the Jews in Rome with a reference to Leviticus 18, explaining that keeping God's "statutes and ordinances" was once the starting point for righteousness but now righteousness is found in faith in Jesus Christ.

Faith in Jesus Christ, open to all peoples, opens salvation to all people.

So then, if faith is the starting point of righteousness and thus salvation, how do people come to faith? What is the mechanism that moves us toward a faithful life? Well, I'm glad you asked.

Prior to his conversion encounter with Jesus, Paul had a very strong sense of vocation. He was convinced that he was to root out the new Jesus movement from the synagogues, as Christianity was not yet separate from Judaism. Paul was one of the earliest persecutors of the first-century Jesus movement. He was good at what he did, and was entirely convinced that God had called him to that task. So after his conversion encounter with Jesus, the new vocation given to Paul was taken on with the same intensity.

This vocation is best seen in this section of his letter to the Romans: proclamation of salvation for all through the life, death, and resurrection of Jesus Christ. This is a vocation that people like me, pastors, are called to but also everyone that claims the Christian faith. From the novice convert to the those who have never missed a daily devotional or weekly worship, all are called to proclaim that through his death and resurrection Jesus opened salvation up to all peoples, and that this is evident in his ministry to people who had been marginalized by the religious leaders of His time.

The saying, "Preach the Gospel and when necessary use words," is attributed to Saint Francis of Assisi. Francis was a Catholic Friar who formed an order to live simply, and follow the teachings of Jesus and walk in Jesus' footsteps. The order still exists today within the Catholic Church and they are known as the Franciscans. (they also wear really cool gray robes that make our albs look pretty lame). It is easy to see how the saying, "Preach the Gospel and when necessary use words," could be attributed to Francis but none of his earliest biographers ever quoted Francis as saying it.

Beyond Francis never saying, "Preach the Gospel and when necessary use words," the statement itself is contradicting. To preach something, according the Merriam Webster, means to deliver something publicly, "advocate earnestly," and "to set forth in a sermon." So by definition, "Preach the Gospel and when necessary use words," is a hard sell.

"Preach the Gospel and when necessary use words," highlights a theological debate that has been occurring amongst Christians for centuries: faith verses works. While on one hand we have Paul telling us we are justified by our faith in Jesus Christ, we find in *The Letter of James* "faith by itself, if it has no works, is dead." This debate has led to Christians comparing and counting the works they do, judging their faithfulness and the faithfulness of others to a checklist of things they think should be done by others. The problem is that, "Preach the Gospel and when necessary use words," along with "faith by itself, if it has no works, is dead," are concerned with social holiness and social holiness while being a byproduct of faith in Jesus Christ is on its own not the Gospel.

The Gospel is not a habit or practice. It is not a list of mission trips must-dos or daily prayer journal habits, but instead the Gospel is a history. Proclamation of the Gospel is the declaration that something happened on a tree on a hill over 2000 years ago and that three days after that something happened something even greater happened.

The Gospel of Jesus Christ is just that the Gospel of Jesus. It is not something we can do because Jesus has already done it.

So it is a both/and situation.

As we heard in our reading from *The Book of Isaiah* God's word provides life, accomplishing that which God wants it to. That is exactly what happened on the cross and in the empty tomb but it is also what happens every time you proclaim that the love poured out on the cross and the power on display in the empty tomb is for all people, without exception.

Any starting point other than the Gospel in Christian proclamation leads us to proof-texting, making the holy scriptures fit into the agenda we are trying to push, which in turn makes the proclamation more about us and less about Jesus. Everyday people get in front of cameras and declare that the Bible says this and because of this now that is justified.

To be clear, Romans 13 is not the starting point for Christian proclamation and because some feel the need to misuse that text the rest of us are left with little choice to but to preach that the saving grace of God is made available to all people because if we do not, those who have not yet heard the Good News of the Gospel will think that Christianity is something it is not. Proof-texting has been and is being used to marginalize, enslave, and imprison people in ways that are entirely contradictory to the Gospel of Jesus Christ. When this happens, we have little choice but to respond by proclaiming that the life, death, and resurrection of Jesus Christ transformed the way we look at the world and thus as Christians the we way we engage the world.

The saving work that we proclaim has been done by Jesus. Words and actions do matter, both are necessary but the former leads to the latter. While faith without works might be dead, works without the Gospel proclamation only point others to the self-righteousness we want to put on display. Proclamation is not about us. It does not start with us and it does not end with us. So when we are stuck starring at a blank page in a notebook or feel as though we do not know what to say, the Good News is that the "work" has been done by Jesus, now we get share it with the world.

Romans 11:25-32 - Razing Hell

Jason Micheli

So that you may not claim to be wiser than you are, brothers and sisters, I want you to understand this mystery: a hardening has come upon part of Israel, until the full number of the Gentiles has come in. And so all Israel will be saved; as it is written, "Out of Zion will come the Deliverer; he will banish ungodliness from Jacob." "And this is my covenant with them, when I take away their sins." As regards the gospel they are enemies of God for your sake; but as regards election they are beloved, for the sake of their ancestors; for the gifts and the calling of God are irrevocable. Just as you were once disobedient to God but have now received mercy because of their disobedience, so they have now been disobedient in order that, by the mercy shown to you, they too may now receive mercy. For God has imprisoned all in disobedience so that he may be merciful to all.

—Romans 11:25-32

Back in the day, before I was the wise and seasoned pastor you see before you, I worked for a couple of years as a chaplain at the maximum security prison in Trenton, New Jersey.

I enjoyed it.

In a lot of ways, the Gospel makes more sense in a place like that than anywhere else. Not to mention, preaching is different when the men hearing you aren't there because their wives or mothers have forced their attendance.

So I enjoyed the prison, but I didn't enjoy everything about the job.

Part of my routine, every week, was to visit and counsel the inmates in solitary confinement.

It was a sticky, hot, dark wing of the prison.

Because every inmate was locked behind a heavy, steel door with just a sliver of thick plexiglass for a window, unlike the rest of the prison, the solitary wing was as silent as a tomb.

Whenever I think of Hell, I think of that place.

But not for the reasons you might expect.

Whenever I visited solitary, the officer on duty was almost always a 50-something Sergeant named Moore.

Officer Moore had a thick, Mike Ditka mustache and coarse sandy hair he combed into a meticulous, greased part. He was tall and strong and, to be honest, intimidating. He had a Marine Corps tattoo on one forearm and a heart with a woman's name on the other arm.

If we weren't in church, I'd also tell you he was a blank-hole.

So ... you get the picture.

Whenever I visited solitary he'd buzz me inside only after I refused to go away. He'd usually be sitting down, gripping the sides of his desk, reading a newspaper.

I hated going there because, every time I did, he'd greet me with heated ridicule.

He'd grumble things like: "Save your breath, preacher, you're wasting your time."

He'd grumble things like: "Do you know what these people did? They don't deserve forgiveness."

He'd grumble things like: "They only listen to you because they've got no one else."

Once, when we gathered for a worship service, I'd invited Officer Moore to join us.

He grumbled that he'd have "nothing to do with a God who'd have anything to do with trash like them" and he refused to come in.

Instead he sat outside with his arm crossed.

The locked prison door between us.

About halfway through my time at the prison, Officer Moore suffered a near fatal heart attack; in fact, he was dead for several minutes before the rescue squad revived him.

I know this because when he returned to work, he told me.

Tried to throw it in my face.

"It's all a sham" he grumbled at me one afternoon.

"I was dead for three minutes. Dead. And you know what I experienced? Nothing. I didn't see any bright light at the end of any tunnel. It was just darkness. Your god? All make believe."

Back then—at the beginning of my ministry, before I was the wise and seasoned pastor you see before you—I tended towards sarcasm.

So even though I don't put much stock in the light at the end of the tunnel cliché, that didn't stop me from saying to Sergeant Moore:

"Maybe you should take that as a warning. Maybe there's no light at the end of the tunnel for *you*."

He grumbled and said: "Don't tell me *you* believe in Hell?"

"What makes you think I *wouldn't* believe in Hell?" I asked, playing with him.

"Oh, since I don't believe in your Jesus, I'm going to Hell? Is that it?"

Officer Moore pushed his chair back and fussed with his collar. He suddenly seemed uncomfortable.

His eyes took a bead on me.

"So what the Hell is Hell like then?" he asked, smirking. "Fire and brimstone, I mean, really?"

"No," I said, "fire, brimstone, gnashing of teeth, those are probably all metaphors."

He let out a sarcastic sigh of relief.

So then I added: "Metaphors for something much worse maybe."

That got his attention.

"Your loving God sends people to a place worse than brimstone just because they don't believe in him?" he asked.

"Who said anything about God sending them there?" I said. "No, I think Hell is a place where the door is locked from the inside.'

Back then, I wasn't the wise and seasoned and mature pastor you see before you, so I didn't mention to him that I'd plagiarized that line from C.S. Lewis.

———

Hell is a place where the door is locked from the inside.

By us.

I said.

Back then.

But is it?

Is that even possible?

"If God is for us, who is against us?" Paul asks three chapters prior to today's text.

If God is for us — all of us

If God is determined to reconcile and redeem all of us

And not only us —

If God is determined to rescue and restore all of creation from its bondage to the Power of Sin, then what could stand in God's way?

"If God is for us, who is against us?" Paul asks back in Romans 8.

If God made each of us and all that is and called it very good — that's Genesis 1.

And if God is determined to make each of us and all that is beautiful again — that's Genesis 12.

If God in Jesus Christ came for all — that's John 1.

If Christ died for all — that's 2 Corinthians 5.15.

If the Judge was judged in your place, once for all — that's Hebrews 10.

And if God raised Jesus from the dead as the first fruit, the first sign, the harbinger of what God intends to do for all of creation — 1 Corinthians 15.

If that's what God intends, then what is to stop God from getting what God wants?

If God's unambiguous aim is the salvation of all, then what ultimately can get in God's way?

Because by definition *nothing* can deny God what God desires. That's 2 Timothy 2.13.

Or, as Paul frames it back in Romans 8: "What can separate us from the love of God in Christ Jesus our Lord? What, in the end, can separate us from God?

And one by one Paul proceeds to eliminate the possibilities:

Hardship. Check.

Injustice. Check.

Persecution. Famine. Check. Check.

Nakedness. Nope.

War. Not it either. It can't separate us from the love of God. None of them.

Not Death. Not Rulers. Not Powers. Neither things present nor things to come. Not anything in all of creation. Nothing can separate us from what God wants to do with us.

Except—

The Apostle Paul does leave one possibility off his list:

Hardship. Injustice. Persecution. Famine. Nakedness. Peril. War. Death. Rulers. Powers.

There is one possibility missing from Paul's list.

One potential disqualifier remains: Us.

Hardship. Injustice. Persecution. Famine. Nakedness. Peril. Sword.

Not any of them can separate us from the love of God in Christ Jesus our Lord, but what about us?

————

What about us? Can we separate ourselves from the love of God?

Can we separate ourselves from God through our unbelief, through our lack of faith, through our disobedient refusal to accept the grace of God in Jesus Christ?

Do we possess that power? Do we possess the ability to separate ourselves forever from the love of God? To slam the door and throw the lock?

Can we really run away and hide forever from a God who's so determined to get us that he chases us all the way to a cross and back?

If Nakedness and Famine and War can't do it, can we?

Can we separate ourselves from God so that the God who desires the salvation of all only ends up with some?

Can we make it so that the God who wants *all* only gets *some*?

Do we have the capacity to keep from God the *everything* God wants?

That's the question Paul takes up next in Romans 9-11 and he does so by turning to the most obvious example available to him.

Israel.

The Jews—those who've received the message of the Gospel and not responded in faith and obedience.

When it comes to unbelievers like them, has the Word of God failed? Paul asks at the beginning of Romans 9.

How are they to be saved by him in whom they have not believed? Paul asks in Romans 10.

It's not really the case that God has rejected God's People, is it? Paul asks at the top of today's chapter.

And just the grammar of that last question gives away the answer. As soon as Paul refers to Israel as *God's* People he's already shown his tell: "By no means!" Paul answers immediately in verse 1.

By no means! God has not rejected God's People!

His chosen People.

The People he's promised, no-strings-attached: "I will be your God and you will be my People."

It's not really the case that God has rejected God's People, is it?

By no means — for if God will break his promise to them, then Paul could've ended his letter back in Romans 8.

And his list could've been a lot shorter.

Who can separate us from the love of God? Well, Paul, it turns out God can separate us from God. God can break his no-strings-attached unconditional covenant promise. God can reject God's People.

So —

Has God rejected God's People?

By no means! is the only possible answer for Paul.

God has not rejected God's People because they reject God's Messiah.

Or rather, in rejecting God's Messiah they have not separated themselves from the love of God.

Because Israel —

They're not responsible for their rejection of God's Messiah.

Paul's whole letter to the Romans has been about what God does not do about what we do, and Paul's focus on the agency of God doesn't change when he turns to God's People in chapters 9-11.

God's People —

They're not responsible for their rejection of God's Messiah.

They're not the acting agents. They're not behind their lack of belief. Their failure of faith is not their fault. They've not decided to disobey.

No.

If God cannot break a no-strings-attached promise, then that leaves only one possibility for Paul.

Israel's rejection of Christ and God's apparent rejection of them — it's God's doing, not their own.

And, Paul says, it fits a pattern of what God has always done:

God choosing Abel over Cain.

God choosing Jacob over Esau. Moses over Pharaoh.

God choosing David over Saul.

God choosing Israel over all the other nations of the earth.

What looks like God's rejection of some in scripture always serves God's election of all.

Even the Father rejecting the Son, "My God, my God, why have you forsaken me?" even that forsaking is for all.

Have God's People stumbled so as to fall away forever from God? Paul asks in verse 11 before he answers in the very same breath: "No!"

Instead their stumbling, their rejection — like Abel instead of Cain, like Sarah instead of Hagar, like Isaac instead of Ishmael — their stumbling is *for* the reconciliation of the whole world, Paul says in verse 15.

The failure of some to believe does not frustrate God's aim to save all.

Let me say that again because it's so paradoxical it can only be Gospel:

The failure of some to believe does not frustrate God's aim to save all.

The failure of some to believe is in fact the means by which God is working even now to show mercy to all.

Paul calls this means a "mystery."

"So that you may not claim to be wiser than you are, brothers and sisters, I want you to understand this mystery: a hardening has come upon some of Israel, until all [the world] has come to God."

Only, in the New Testament, the word mystery doesn't refer to something still unknown to us. In the New Testament, a mystery isn't something that leaves you still in the dark scratching your head.

In the New Testament, a mystery is a *secret that's been revealed* to us by God — a mystery is a secret that can be told.

As when the Apostle Paul tells the Corinthians "Behold, I tell you a mystery ..." and then Paul proclaims the secret that's been revealed to us: "We will not die ... we will be changed ... for on the day of Resurrection we will be raised ... that which is perishable will become imperishable."

Likewise, here Paul writes to the Church at Rome: "I want you to understand this *secret that's been revealed to us...*"

The mystery—the mystery is that God has chosen some for disobedience so that others might obey.

The mystery is that God has chosen some for disbelief so that others might believe.

The opened secret is that God has chosen ungodliness for some so that others might find God.

"...a hardening has come upon them..." Paul says.

Note the passive voice.

Notice, it's not: "They've hardened their hearts."

It's come upon them. God is doing it.

Just as you believe in Jesus Christ solely by the gracious work of God upon you, so too they disbelieve because of the work of God upon them.

A hardening has come upon some so that all might come to God, Paul says.

And then in the next verse, Paul declares: "... so *all* Israel will be saved."

Pantes is the word and Paul doesn't qualify it all.

It means *all*.

Notice what Paul doesn't say—

He doesn't say all Israel will believe. He doesn't say all Israel will confess Jesus Christ and *thereby* be saved.

He just says all Israel will be saved. Your belief, their unbelief —it's a mystery.

It's all God's doing.

Your belief is not your doing. Their unbelief is not their doing. It's all God's doing.

So—

Those who reject the love of God in Jesus Christ, those who reject the Gospel, they're not enemies of God. God has made them enemies of the Gospel *for you.*

For your sake: "... God has imprisoned *some* in disobedience so that God might be merciful to *all.*"

You see, for Paul the danger isn't that unbelievers could ever separate themselves from the love of God in Christ Jesus; the danger is that believers like you will draw that conclusion.

A few days after our conversation about Hell, I left in Officer Moore's mailbox a copy of a book, C.S. Lewis's *The Great Divorce.*

It's a fable about the residents of Hell taking a bus trip to Heaven. They're given the option to stay but, one by one, they choose to turn and go back.

I had dog-eared some pages and highlighted some text for Officer Moore, hoping we could talk about it the next time I saw him.

Specifically, I highlighted these words:

It is not a question of God "sending us" to hell. In the end, there are only two kinds of people: those who say to God, "Your will be done," and those to whom God says, "Your will be done."

I left the book in his mailbox.

A week later I went to solitary to see if he wanted to talk.

As always he refused to buzz me in but this time when I mentioned I was there to talk to him, he didn't give in. He wouldn't let me in.

I asked if he read the book.

Not saying anything, he got up and walked to the entrance door, his body was one big snarl.

He slid the book between the bars.

"A whole lot of nonsense" he grumbled at me.

And then he told me to go the Hell away.

Back then, I wasn't the wise and seasoned and quick-witted pastor you see before you today. To be honest, back then I hadn't ever read the Apostle Paul's Letter to the Romans.

Because if I had I could've told him.

You're right, I could've said to him. It is a whole lot of nonsense. C.S. Lewis might've known a lot about lions and wardrobes and Turkish Delight, but he didn't know jack about this secret that's been revealed to us: the mystery.

The mystery of our disobedience.

You're right, I could've, should've, would've said to him.

Hell is where the door is locked from the inside by us?! That's a whole lot of nonsense.

Not only is it idolatrous, for it imagines a Self whose desires are stronger than God's desire.

It completely misses the mystery that's been revealed to us:

That salvation is the work of God where even our "No" to God serves God's ultimate "Yes" to us.

Even our "No" to God is itself the work of God working towards what God wants for all.

You're right, I could've shot back at the Sergeant.

It is a whole lot of nonsense.

How could we ever separate ourselves forever from the love of God in Jesus Christ when even the disobedience of some is part of God's plan for all?

God is bigger than our badness.

We can't lock Hell's doors from the inside because ultimately the work of God is going to make even our disobedience and disbelief work in our favor because of his favor, his unmerited favor, which is his grace.

The disobedience and disbelief of some is only temporary.

God will banish all ungodliness.

God will turn disobedience to obedience. God will turn disbelief into belief.

God will transform unfaithfulness to faithfulness as surely as he can bring life from death.

And in the meantime—I could've told him.

There is nothing that can separate you from the love of God in Christ Jesus our Lord—whether you like it or not.

There is nothing about you that can separate you from the love of God in Jesus Christ.

There is nothing in all of creation—not war, not famine, not powers or persecution, not even you—there is nothing in all of creation that can separate you from the love of God because everything in creation is a work of God's grace.

Even your disbelief.

Maybe you can lock the door for a time, I could've said to him, but in the end God will raze even Hell to get what God wants: you.

God wants you.

———

Of course, if I had told him all that back then, he would've just grumbled some more.

If all are saved, no matter what, then what's the point? He might've replied.

Why should I bother following your Jesus?

Back then I wasn't the wise and seasoned preacher you see before you. I wouldn't have had the presence of mind to say to him what I'd say today:

What's the point if all are saved?

What's the point of being first rather than last?

Why be found rather than lost?

Why know the truth rather than live in ignorance?

Why be fully human?

What's the point?

To ask the question is to miss the point.

Romans 12:1-2 - We Are The Stories We Tell

Taylor Mertins

I appeal to you therefore, brothers and sister, by the mercies of God, to present your bodies as a living sacrifice, holy and acceptable to God, which is your spiritual worship. Do not be conformed to this world, but be transformed by the renewing of your minds, so that you may discern what is the will of God – what is good and acceptable and perfect. Do not be conformed to this world, but be transformed by the renewing of your minds.

- Romans 12.1-2

Years ago there was a young man fresh out of seminary, ready and eager to begin serving his first appoint in the United Methodist Church. He had taken all the right classes, learned from the best professors, and was excited about finally embarking on the ministry he had imagined for so long.

All he knew about his church was the name, John Wesley UMC, and the location, off in the middle of nowhere Georgia.

The young man was so anxious about the appointment that when he first got to town, a few days before his first Sunday, he got in his car and drove straight to the church. But when he arrived at what he thought was the address there was no church, so he doubled back and drove down the empty road until he found a disheveled looking building with the biggest and most unruly tree he had ever seen blocking the marquee and most of the structure.

The church clearly needed work: a new roof, new paint, new everything, it even had a bell tower without a bell. But above all it needed to have the tree uprooted. The young man stood there on the front lawn looking at the tree and the wheels started clicking in his mind... **He thought that if he took the tree down, individuals from the community would be able to see the church and the sign from the main road and they might even get a couple extra visitors on his first Sunday.**

So instead of going back to the parsonage to unpack all of his belongings and get settled, he went straight to the box with his chain saw and he went back to John Wesley UMC.

Hours later, with sweat dripping down his brow, the young pastor stood proudly in front of the church that was now completely visible from the road with the old gnarled tree perfectly arranged in neat even logs stacked in the back.

A few days passed and the young pastor was sitting in the study at the parsonage preparing his very first sermon in his very first church when the phone rang. It was the District Superintendent and the pastor briefly thought that maybe his boss was calling to congratulate him on the quick work with the tree and the beauty of the totally visible church, but the DS said, "**I hope you haven't finished unpacking yet, because you're being sent to a different church.**"

You see: the church was named John Wesley UMC for a reason. Back in the 1730s John Wesley had planted that tree during his mission to the colony of Georgia and the community built a church around the tree to commemorate where the founder of the movement had once served. For centuries the tree stood as a reminder of all that Wesley stood for, the roots were reminiscent of the need for a deep love for the scriptures, and its shade was loved like the mustard bush from the time of Jesus.

And that young, foolish, and brazen pastor had chopped it down to the ground.

Stories are remarkably important. They contain everything about who we were, who we are, and who we can be. Stories held within a community help to shape the ways we interact with one another and how we understand what it means to live in this world. We tell stories to make people laugh, to teach lessons, and to hold dear the most important elements of existence.

Stories are remarkably important. I've been saying some version of that sentence in every sermon over the last 4 years. It's what I started with, and it's what I'm ending with.

We are the stories we tell.

By my rough calculations I've preached over 250 times while serving St. John's and written about as many devotionals. I've traveled hundreds and hundreds of miles, read countless books, and gone to the hospital enough time that a few of the security guards will wave me into the ER without having to ask who I am.

I've gone to more meetings than I ever thought possible, compiled annual budgets I though we could never meet (though we always did), and led bible studies that have addressed almost every book of the bible.

And in all of this, I've written close to a million words in four years. Between the sermons and the studies, the devotionals and the prayers, even the chapel times and the epistles, nearly one million words.

All of those million words, in whatever context they appeared, they have been my attempt at saying these words: **We are the stories we tell.**

I could tell you the story about how the first time I ever walked into this sanctuary it was late in the evening on Good Friday in 2013 and no one could figure out how to turn the lights on. I groped around this room in the dark hoping to have a sense of what it looked like and left none the wiser. I love that story because it became indicative of our time together: rediscovering the light of Christ that burns in our lives.

Or I could tell you the story about how the first time I ever led the Children's Message during worship I realized that I was closer in age to the kids sitting on the steps than to the vast majority of you folk sitting in the pews. I love that story because it quickly embodied how this church needed to discover it's multi-generational gifts and people of all different ages have really grown closer together.

Or I could tell you the story about how on my very first Sunday I remembered to do everything except I forgot to give the ushers the offerings plates. It was good for a refreshing laugh that first worship service and I love that story because in it we learned, as a church, to stop worrying about the offering plate and instead we began to believe that the Lord would provide, and the Lord has provided ever since.

We, preachers and laypeople alike, tell stories in order that they might be remembered. We tell children about George Washington and his tree so that they will tell the truth. We tell high school students about political elections from the past so that they might cast informed votes in the future. We tell older adults about what our children have been up to so that they might live a little through them.

We tell stories because we want them to be remembered.
But recently I was reading a book by Ellen Davis and she believes that a successful sermon is one that isn't remembered. Sounds strange right? I've stood in this pulpit for four years in the hopes that you might actually remember what I said. But after reading that part of her book, I went through the archives and I came across a ton of sermons that I barely remember writing, let alone preaching.

A forgotten sermon is successful because we have to keep showing up Sunday after Sunday to hear again the story that makes us who we are.

If one sermon was capable of proclaiming all that the bible has to tell, all of the life of Jesus Christ, all of God's glory, all of the fellowship of the Spirit, then we would never come back and our lives would be perfect from then on.

But that's not the way our lives work!
The goal of preaching, and of good story telling, is the hope that people won't remember what you said. The goal should be that the next time someone turns to that part of the Bible it will say a little more to him or her. **The purpose of the church, of doing worship week after week, is to give the bible a little more room to shine.**

Now, don't get me wrong… I hope you won't forget me. I hope you will think back over these last years with fondness. I'm even bold to hope that you might remember some of my sermons. **But more than that, I hope when you open up your bibles, the story of God with God's people shines a light in your life, regardless of whomever the person was that stood in this pulpit.**

Because today, the world is full of stories, competing narratives vying for our allegiance. It is almost impossible to go anywhere or do anything without someone or something telling us how we are supposed to understand the world.

And Paul dismisses all of it. Do not be conformed to this world but be transformed by the renewing of your mind. Do not let your favorite reality television show dictate how you understand others, don't let the news channel send you to the corner to cower in fear, do not let your political proclivities limit your relationship with those who are of a different opinion. Instead, be transformed by the renewing of your minds. Tell the story that is our story! Jesus Christ and him crucified!

Be transformed by the renewing of your mind. God transforms our lives whenever we gather in this place for worship and whenever we tell the story. The story of God in Christ reconciling himself to the World is what transforms us into the very people God is calling us to be.

According to the world, the church is in between a rock and a hard place. Mainline Protestant Christianity is floundering in the United States, people are no longer attending church like they once did, offering plates feel lighter and lighter. Christianity has lost its status in the political arena, we are becoming biblically illiterate, and young people are disappearing from the fabric of church.

The church is between a rock and a hard place.

Thanks be to God then that Jesus Christ is the solid rock upon which we stand! We don't have to be conformed to the ways of the world! We get to be transformed by the renewing of our minds by telling the story that is our story!

Jesus does not work according to the ways of the world. He does not say bring me your votes and your mortgages and your perfect families. Jesus says, bring me your burdens and I will bring you rest.

Jesus does not tell us to earn all that we can and save all that we can. Jesus tells us to give away all we can.

Jesus does not say that our religious convictions are private and something to keep to ourselves. Jesus tells us to go tell it on the mountain and share the Good News.

Jesus does not look at our outward appearance and say you're too fat, or short, or tall, or dumb, or slow, or strange. Jesus looks into our hearts and says, **"You are mine and I am thine."**

This church, St. John's, is on the precipice of a great journey; you're about to receive a new pastor. But at the same time, this is nothing new. **This is what the church is! It is the place where disciples gather to hear the story over and over and over again.**

The stories of the world will never compare to the actions of God in the world through Jesus Christ. Whether you're a brother or a sister, mother or father, republican or democrat, rich or poor, old or young, none of those narratives, none of those identities, none of those stories compare with what it means to follow Jesus.

According to the ways of the world the church is in a difficult place. But I'm not worried about any of that, I'm not worried about anything because my hope is not in me, it's not in Pastor Chuck Cole, my hope is not built on the ways of the world. My hope is built on nothing less than Jesus's blood and righteousness. Christ is the solid rock upon which this church stands. Jesus Christ is Lord and that means that the ways of the world crumble away when compared to the foundation made manifest in God in the flesh.

We are here in this place to share our stories with one another in order that we might learn more about how we are caught up in God's great story. The ways of the world are nothing but sinking sand, they falter and flounder, they creak and groan, but God's story is eternally unshakable.

Be transformed by the renewing of your minds! Remember that Jesus is Lord! Keep the faith! Let the stories of scripture wash over you like the waters of baptism. Feast at this table like the disciples did with Jesus long ago!

Do not be conformed to this world, but be transformed by the renewing of your minds! To God be the Glory!

Romans 12:1-2, 9-21 - What the Therefore Is There For

Jason Micheli

I appeal to you therefore, brothers and sisters, by the mercies of God, to present your bodies as a living sacrifice, holy and acceptable to God, which is your spiritual worship. Do not be conformed to this world, but be transformed by the renewing of your minds, so that you may discern what is the will of God—what is good and acceptable and perfect. Let love be genuine; hate what is evil, hold fast to what is good; love one another with mutual affection; outdo one another in showing honor. Do not lag in zeal, be ardent in spirit, serve the Lord. Rejoice in hope, be patient in suffering, persevere in prayer. Contribute to the needs of the saints; extend hospitality to strangers. Bless those who persecute you; bless and do not curse them. Rejoice with those who rejoice, weep with those who weep. Live in harmony with one another; do not be haughty, but associate with the lowly; do not claim to be wiser than you are. Do not repay anyone evil for evil, but take thought for what is noble in the sight of all. If it is possible, so far as it depends on you, live peaceably with all. Beloved, never avenge yourselves, but leave room for the wrath of God; for it is written, "Vengeance is mine, I will repay, says the Lord." No, "if your enemies are hungry, feed them; if they are thirsty, give them something to drink; for by doing this you will heap burning coals on their heads." Do not be overcome by evil, but overcome evil with good.

—Romans 12:1-2, 9-21

Pay attention to the passive voice:

"Our society is broken, pretty much, but there will be a time when these times will be made right."

"…these times will be made right" said the principal of Goose Creek High School in Charleston, South Carolina.

"…these times will be made right" he said just days after Dylann Roof stormed into Mother Emmanuel AME Church and shot 9 parishioners gathered for bible study. One of the nine victims was the track coach at Goose Creek High School.

"…these times will be made right."

Which is to say, despite the brokenness we can see everywhere an unseen agency is at work, making right. Or as Paul would say, rectifying.

Only four days after Dylann Roof stormed into Emmanuel AME and left six black women and three black men in a bloody pile in the church basement, the leaders of the congregation concluded the only way to press forward was for them to go back to exactly what they'd done before, to do the Sunday after that shooting what they had done the Sunday previous.

Worship the Lord Jesus Christ.

Proclaim the Gospel. The Gospel that Paul says is the rectifying power of God unleashed in our world (1.16-17).

Preaching that Sunday at Mother Emmanuel AME Church, Reverend Norvel Goff, an elder in the African Methodist Episcopal Church, proclaimed: "through our proclamation of the Gospel on this day a message will be sent to Satan."

Note the passive voice again: "through our proclamation…a message will be sent."

The worshipers at Emmanuel Church were not the ones sending the message.

Later in his sermon, his voice roaring, Reverend Goff added: "Something wants to divide us—black and brown and white—but no weapon formed against us shall prosper."

Notice—he didn't say Dylann Roof wanted to divide us. He didn't say racists and bigots want to divide us. He said something wants to divide us—there's another agency at work in the world.

Speaking of that other agency, that same Sunday, outside the church, the Reverend Brandon Bowers, who is white and the pastor of Awaken Church, said: "What the Enemy intended for evil, God is using —God is using us—for good."

He said Enemy with a capital E—even the *NY Times* caught it.

And he did not say we're using this for good.

Pay attention to the passive: "God is using us for good."

We're being used by God for good.

The service at Mother Emmanuel AME Church began with a hymn: "You are the Source of my strength, you are the strength of my life."

Meanwhile, while they sang at Emmanuel AME, the family of 21 year old Dylann Roof worshiped at St. Paul's Lutheran Church in Columbia, South Carolina.

The pastor of St. Paul's read the names of the victims and the congregation prayed for them and their families. The victimizer's family prayed for the victims and their families.

About the victimizer's family, the pastor of St. Paul told his congregation later: "They are shattered but through their faith they are being made strong."

"...they are being made strong."

"...these times will be made by right."

———

Pay attention to the passive:

"I appeal to you therefore, brothers and sisters, by the mercies of God, to present your bodies as a living sacrifice...Do not be conformed to this world, but be transformed by the renewing of your minds...

Let love be genuine; hate what is evil, hold fast to what is good; love one another with mutual affection...Do not lag in zeal, be ardent in spirit...Rejoice in hope, be patient in suffering, persevere in prayer...

Bless those who persecute you; bless and do not curse them... do not be haughty...do not claim to be wiser than you are. Do not repay anyone evil for evil...if your enemies are hungry, feed them; if they are thirsty, give them something to drink...overcome evil with good."

"I appeal to you therefore...by the mercies of God...do not be conformed...but be transformed by the renewing of your minds."

If you don't understand what the therefore is there for, not only do you miss Paul's point here you mishear this passage as bad news instead of good, as burdensome rather than freeing.

Because, let's face it—

Genuine, 100% of the time, love
Unflagging zeal
Patience in suffering

Perseverance in prayer
Feeding your enemies

I've been here almost 13 years and I don't know any of you who score better than a D on this long list of attributes of what transformation looks like. I'd bet the house that behind closed doors Pope Francis doesn't do better than a B-.

I mean, half of you can't even get along on Facebook, let alone blessing those who curse you. This is DC—a lot of you make your livelihood claiming to be wiser than you really are.

"Do not be haughty?" So long as Donald Trump is in office that's an impossible command for some of you.

Assuming it's a command, that is.

If you don't know what the therefore is there for, you'll mishear this passage.

You won't hear it as Gospel. You'll hear it—if you're honest enough to admit it—as a guilt trip. You'll hear it as a To Do list of musts and shoulds, as a prescription of what we have to do.

Without the therefore there, you'll hear Paul saying: A real transformed Christian looks like this...a genuine Christian must do this...must love enemies, must bless those who curse them, must be patient in suffering and ardent about their faith.

No.

That's what the therefore is there for.

The therefore signals that what comes next depends upon what came before.

The therefore signals that what proceeds is possible only because of what preceded.

The therefore signals that what follows is a part of everything prior.

Or, in other words, chapter 12 comes after chapter 11.

Chapter 12 comes after chapter 8 and chapter 6 and chapter 5 and 3 and 1.

The therefore is there for you to remember that what comes next here in chapter 12 continues and concludes what has come before.

Just before this, the verse that sets up this therefore—it's a doxology. It's a song of praise, thanking God for the work of God to save all of God's creation (11.33-36).

And before that, Paul has said that even the disbelief of some is a part of God's work to show mercy to all. Before that, Paul has said that the all-ness of God's saving work includes not just creatures like you and me but all of creation.

All of creation because all of creation, Paul has said before, is in captivity to the Power of Sin with a capital S. A Power that, just before, Paul made synonymous with the Power of Death with a capital D.

A Power, Paul said before that, whose power we are all under such that not one of us can free ourselves. We have no power against this Power. We're prisoners, Paul has said before.

Which gets back to what Paul said just before that, at the very beginning of his argument (and remember, it is all one, long argument). In his thesis statement at the beginning, before the therefore and everything else, Paul announced that his letter is about what God is doing:

"For I am not ashamed of the Gospel, for in it the rectifying power of God is invading [the world]."

You can only invade territory held by an Enemy.

The Gospel is the Power of God to take God's world back from the Enemy who binds it. The Gospel, Paul has said, is the means by which God takes God's world back from the One who holds it captive.

Pay attention to the present tense.

The Gospel isn't about what God did.

The Gospel is what God does.

Everything that has come before the therefore has been about God's doing.

You didn't invite Jesus into your heart.

God has poured God's love into your heart through the Holy Spirit, Paul has said.

You didn't journey to God.

God has transferred you from the dominion of Sin into the dominion of grace.

You didn't decide to become a new you.

God killed off your old self—you have died with Christ—and now you are in Christ.

You didn't sign up to serve God—God has set you free from slavery to Sin and Death and made you instead a slave of righteousness.

It's all been about what God does.

———

So, why should we suppose that when he gets to this point in his letter Paul is suddenly talking about us, about what we do?

What the therefore is there for is to remind you that what comes next describes what God is doing, not what we do.

It's proclamation not exhortation.

It's indicative not imperative.

The therefore is there so you don't mistake this as a prescription of what we must do: We must be genuine in love. We must be patient in suffering. We must be zealous for God all the time. We must bless those who curse us and love our enemies.

If there's a must or a should or a have-to in your sentences, you're not speaking Gospel.

The therefore is there for you to know this is not a prescription of who you must be or what you must do. It's a description of who Jesus Christ is and what God is doing.

Pay attention to the passive: "I appeal to you therefore…by the mercies of God…do not be conformed…but be transformed by the renewing of your minds."

We're not the ones doing the transforming.

The therefore is there for you to see that this transformation isn't up to us. You're not left to your lonesome to live up to impossible ideals. The point of this passage isn't that you have to become a new you; it's that you are being made new.

By God.

By the mercies of God, Paul says.

That's not a throwaway religious cliche.

The word Paul uses there, *dia*, refers to the instrumentality of God. Paul is saying that only by the merciful activity of God upon you can you be conformed not to this world but transformed into conformity to Jesus Christ.

That's different.

That's different than Paul simply telling you to emulate and imitate Jesus.

Jesus didn't even have an easy time being Jesus; how could you possibly emulate and imitate him?

No, Paul's not exhorting you to imitate Jesus.

Paul's already told you before, back in chapter 6, by faith and by baptism—by God—you *now* are in Jesus Christ. He doesn't mean that as a metaphor.

You are in Jesus Christ.

And now—therefore—Paul is telling you, God is shaping you into Christ likeness.

Patience in suffering. Blessing those who curse you. Perseverance in prayer. Genuine love. This isn't a To Do list or a Christian Code of Conduct. They're not exhortations or expectations. They're attributes of Christ.

He's describing the mind of Christ.

The mind according to which God is at work to conform us.

"I appeal to you therefore...by the mercies of God...do not be conformed...but be transformed by the renewing of your minds."

Pay attention to the language.

That word renewing—it's *anakainosis*. It means literally "completely taken over."

God is at work to transform you. To conform you to Christ.

To completely take over your mind with the mind of Christ.

What Paul says here is what Paul says to the Corinthians: "God made Jesus to be Sin who knew no sin (why?) so that (therefore) we might become the righteousness of God."

What Paul says here is what Paul says to the Philippians: "...the God who began a good work in you will in the fullness of time bring it to completion." Not, *you now have to bring it to completion.* God will bring it to completion.

What Paul says here is what Paul said at the very beginning of this letter:

The Gospel, what we announce in Word and Sacrament—it is the power of Almighty God to invade, to completely take over, until you are rectified, put right, according to the mind of Christ in whose image you are made.

And through you...the world.

"...these times will be made right."

———

Pay attention to the passive.

Last May, Dennis and I attended Hedy's graduation from Wesley Theological Seminary, held at the National Cathedral.

The pastor of Emmanuel AME Church in Charleston, killed by Dylann Roof, would've been in the graduating class.

They awarded his degree posthumously, and when it came time for Reverend Pinckney's name to be read, they invited his wife Jennifer forward to receive his diploma and to speak.

She acknowledged that the ceremony was a bittersweet moment for her. She painted a picture of her husband asleep in his man cave, his coursework still on his lap. And then she confessed that she'd had no idea what to say to those gathered there in the cathedral.

She'd had no idea what to say.

'But then,' she said, 'I was hit with the words to share.'

I was hit.

By God. By the Holy Spirit.

And what followed was plain and unremarkable, but it was powerful — more so than the sermon that had come before, a sermon that had been all exhortation, an exhausting litany of musts and shoulds.

But what Jennifer Pinkney from Emmanuel AME Church said was powerful not because of the pathos of the moment nor for the profundity of her words.

It was powerful because she had reminded us — testified to us — that God is real.

God is living.

Acting.

At work: "...I was hit with what to say..."

———

Look —

You can't become unflagging in your zeal by exerting more zeal.

You don't persevere in prayer by practicing prayer.

Your love doesn't become genuine through effort.

You don't achieve patience in suffering by enduring it.

Blessing those who curse you doesn't come about by you biting your tongue.

You can forgive 70 x 7 times but if it takes in your heart even one of those times it's not your own doing.

You don't walk in newness of life because you set out to do so.

You don't become lovers of enemies by trying—neither will they cease to be your enemy because you've attempted to love them.

None of it is possible for you to do.

But all of it is possible for the Living God to do in you.

The therefore is there for you to remember that the Christian life is pointless if the God we serve is not a Living God.

The therefore is there for you to remember that Christianity is bigger than simply doing the things Jesus did because you can't do any of the things Jesus did if God did not raise him from the dead to conform and transform you.

And sure that takes different kind of patience, sure that sounds messier and slower and more frustrating than if Paul just handed us a simple To Do List of Musts and Shoulds.

But our understanding of the Gospel, our understanding of what it means to be a Christian, should at least require that Jesus Christ is alive and at work in the world.

———

The Sunday after Dylann Roof shot nine at Emmanuel AME Church in Charleston, members of Citadel Baptist Church, members of a white Southern Baptist Church with a long and complicated relationship with racism walked the mere steps from their church to Emmanuel Church and placed purple daises around the front of Emmanuel.

The Reverend David Walker, pastor of Citadel Baptist, explained the gesture thus. Pay attention to the passive:

"Something compelled us to do this…"

Christ is Risen indeed.

Romans 13:1 - The Separation of Church and State

Taylor Mertins

Let every person be subject to the governing authorities; for there is no authority except from God, and those authorities that exist have been instituted by God.

- Romans 13.1

The Church and the State have a long and complicated relationship. Like a number of romantic couples from popular TV shows, think Ross and Rachel, Sam and Diane, Jim and Pam, Luke and Lorelai, and even Kermit and Miss Piggy, the "will they/won't they" question of their relationships has happened over and over and over again.

It began during the days of Jesus. A wandering and poor Jew developed a following that threatened the power dynamics of the Jewish leadership and the Roman Empire. His *actions* might have appeared innocuous, feeding the multitudes by the sea, healing the blind, walking on water, but what he *said* terrified those in power: "**The last shall be first and the first shall be last,**" sounds the beginning of a call to revolution.

And for living and healing and preaching the way he did, Jesus was nailed to a cross. But three days later he rose from the dead. The Christian church began in the wake of Jesus' resurrection, the power of the Good News of God's triumph over death spread throughout the region and small groups gathered together to worship the Lord Jesus Christ. The book of Acts, and Paul's letters, help us to see how the story traveled and took hold of the communities where it was received. Lives were transformed; the gospel spread, and the kingdom began to become incarnate.

But whatever the church stood for, and whatever the state stood for, was very different.

Most of what we know about the early church comes from scripture. Which is to say, we know what the church thought about the church. However, we do have some idea of what the state thought about the church. Pliny the Younger was the governor of Pontus (Asia Minor) from 111 to 113 CE. During his rule he wrote to the Roman Emperor Trajan about the Christians in his community in response to their unwillingness to worship the Emperor: "They [the Christians] asserted, however, that the sum and substance of their fault of error had been that they were accustomed to meet on a fixed day before dawn and sing responsively a hymn to Christ as to a god, and to bind themselves by oath, not to some crime, but not to commit fraud, theft, or adultery, not falsify their trust, not to refuse to return a trust when called upon to do so. When this was over, it was their custom to depart and to assemble again to partake of food – but ordinary and innocent food."

The first Christians were strange, with their singing songs to a man who died on a cross, and sharing bread and wine, and promising to be good and trustworthy. How bizarre. And for nearly 300 years they were persecuted, abused, and killed for following Jesus. The state, Rome, resented the Christians and their weirdness. **They refused to bow down to worship the Emperor like everyone else. Instead they believed some guy named Jesus was Lord. And for that, they were punished.**

But then things changed.

In the year 312 CE something happened that forever affected the relationship between the church and the state. I cannot overemphasize this point enough; it changed everything. The story goes that emperor Constantine was preparing his troops for a battle against a rebellion from within the empire, and on the night before the battle he had a vision of the Greek letters Chi (X) and a Rho (P) in the sky and the words, "in this sign you will conquer." From this vision Constantine ordered all of his troops to be marked with the Chi-Rho, which looks like the symbol on the right hand page of your bulletin. Chi and Rho are the first two letters of Christos (the Greek version of "Messiah"). After doing so, Constantine's army won a decisive victory and he entered Rome shortly thereafter as the undisputed Emperor. The battle gave him complete control of the Western Roman Empire and it paved the way for Christianity to become the dominant faith.

The very next year Constantine issued the Edict of Milan, which made Christianity an officially recognized and tolerated religion in the Roman Empire. Within a dozen years, he called for the Council of

Nicaea, which was the first attempt to attain a consensus in the church through an assembly representing all of Christendom.

From a vision of two Greek letters in the sky, Christians went from being persecuted and murdered, to being part of the state religion.

And now we fast-forward to today, to the United States, to a country founded on the principles of religious freedom, tolerance, and the Separation of Church and State. After centuries of the church and state co-mingling to a frightening degree, the founders decided to move in a different direction. After being persecuted for their different religious convictions they envisioned a new way forward. Recognizing that this place was, and could continue to be, a melting pot of differing ideologies, the forefathers articulated a political system whereby the state could not control religion, nor could religion control the state, and that those two things would find their fullest potential while being completely separated.

Constantine's vision of conquering under the sign of Christ was over, and the time of secularism began.

Paul, writing to the Christians in Rome, said, **"Be subject to the governing authorities."** This is to say, follow the laws of the land, pay your taxes, be good citizens. Paul's words echo through the centuries and reverberate here in this sanctuary: Do as the country tells you to do. If you're called to serve in the military, go to war. If its time for a presidential election, vote with your conscience. If the government says there's a separation of church and state, keep it that way.

And Jesus, speaking to his disciples said, **"This is my commandment, that you love one another as I have loved you... If the world hates you, be aware that it hated me before it hated you. If you belonged to the world, the world would love you as its own. Because you do not belong to the world, but I have chosen you out of the world – therefore the world hates you."** Jesus' words echo through the centuries and reverberate here in this sanctuary: Following me means acting like me. If people are being persecuted, you are to love them with every fiber of your being. If the government starts belittling people for what they believe, you need to stand up for the oppressed. If you feel called to live like a disciple, prepare yourself to be hated by the world.

These two scriptures from Romans and John contain the tension of what it means to be a Christian in the United States. We constantly wrestle between being subject to the governing authorities and pushing back against the governing authorities. We wrestle between what it means to love the world and what it means to be hated by the world. We, as disciples, live in the world but we are not of the world. We may be citizens of the United States, but our truest citizenship is in heaven.

Years ago there was a civil case raised against an organization for displaying a nativity scene on public property. Because of the separation of Church and State, the concerned citizen believed the nativity scene had to be removed. However, when the matter was brought to trial, the court ruled in favor of the Christian display. The reasoning was that because the nativity scene was next to Rudolph the Red-Nosed Reindeer, Frosty the Snowman, and Santa Claus, it had every right to be there. Christians across the country rejoiced when the matter was settled and celebrated what they thought was a decisive victory for the church.

But was it? Should we celebrate a time when the nativity is one of many signs of the holiday? Or should we savor its sacredness? Do we want the nativity to be the same as holiday cartoons, or do we want it to symbolize the profound incarnation of God in the flesh being born in a manger?

A few years ago there was another civil case raised against a baker for refusing to bake a cake for a gay couple's wedding. Because of the freedom of religion, the baker believed it was within his right to refuse service to people who went against his religious convictions. The matter went to trial and the judge ruled that the baker unlawfully and illegally discriminated the couple for their sexual orientation. Christians across the country protested when the matter was settled, and vehemently opposed the ruling.

Were they right? Should Christians support the freedom to pick and choose who they serve? Or should they follow the command to love the way Jesus loved? Do we want the church to be connected with the religious liberty that isolates particular people, or do we want to go against the conventions of fanatical Christianity and love people regardless of any particular identity?

The separation of the Church and the State is a good thing because for too long the state controlled the church. The Constantinian revolution was certainly responsible for spreading Christianity across the globe, but it also led to things like the Crusades and the Inquisition. Constantine co-opted the church for the role of government in such a way that it limited the qualities that made Christians strange, and instead made them normative. Gone were the days when people lived by the convictions of Christ, and instead they went to church because that's what they were expected to do.

But the era of Constantine did not die when our nation was founded. Though we articulate beliefs like the Separation of Church and State, it still says, **"in God** we trust" on our national currency, children still pledge their allegiance to the flag and country **under God** every morning before school starts, and we still have many courts where we must place our hands on a bible and are asked, "Do you swear to tell the truth, the whole truth, and nothing but the truth, so help you **God**?"

So perhaps now is the time, the best time, to recover those qualities that will make the world hate us. Not the qualities of religious bigotry and prejudice that for too long have dominated the state's view of the church. But the qualities of Christ-like love that drive the state crazy. Like refusing to bow and worship our country and our politicians as if they were gods, and instead worshipping the risen Lord. Like gathering together on a day set apart to hold ourselves accountable to honesty, truthfulness, and peace. Like sitting before a table of ordinary food of bread and wine that becomes the extraordinary gift of body and blood.

We are in the world, but we are not of the world. We might have national citizenship, but our true Lord is Jesus Christ. We are like strangers living in a strange land. Amen.

Romans 13:11-14 - Wake Up!

Taylor Mertins

Besides this, you know what time it is, how it is now the moment for you to wake from sleep. For salvation is nearer to us now than when we became believers; the night is far gone, the day is near. Let us then lay aside the works of darkness and put on the armor of light; let us live honorably as in the day, not in reveling and drunkenness, not in debauchery and licentiousness, not in quarreling and jealousy. Instead, put on the Lord Jesus Christ, and make no provision for the flesh, to gratify its desires.

-Romans 13.11-14

On April 4th, 1742, Charles Wesley came up for appointment as university preacher in St. Mary's in London. Charles preached from Ephesians 5.14 which reads, **"Awake, thou that sleepest, and arise from the dead, and Christ shall give thee light."**

Now, just for context sake, Charles Wesley was the younger brother of John Wesley, the primary founder of the Methodist renewal movement that eventually led to the formation of the United Methodist Church. Both brothers believed that, at the time, the Church of England was losing a sense of purpose and needed to be renewed. They were strongly rooted within their church structure, but they considered their ministries to be caught up in spreading scriptural holiness throughout the land. While John was known for his organization and preaching, Charles was known for his ability to write hymns; some of his more celebrated hymns are sung on a regular basis in many churches: **Christ the Lord is Risen Today, Come Thou Long Expected Jesus, Hark! the Herald Angels Sing, O for a Thousand Tongues to Sing,** to name a few.

So, Charles found himself invited to preach in front of a university audience that he largely believed had lost sight of what it meant to be Christian in the world. Those in attendance that day were far more consumed with the "academic pursuits" of Christianity rather than a deep and inward sense of what it meant to be forgiven and loved.

Like many young and naive pastors, Charles preached a sermon filled with a barrage of frightening assumptions and left many in attendance frustrated, angry, and ignorant.

Here are a few of his lines, adapted for our contemporary period: **Wake up!** Everyone of you, wake up out of your dreams of worldly happiness. What is the state of your soul? If God required you to die right now while I am preaching, are you ready to meet death and judgement? Have you fought the good fight and kept the faith? Have you secured the one thing needful? Have you recovered the image of God, even righteousness and true holiness? Are you clothed in Christ? Do you know that God dwells in you by his Spirit that he has given to you? Have you received the Holy Spirit? Or do you even know if there is a Holy Spirit at all? If any of these questions offend you, be assured that you are not a Christian nor do you desire to be one. Indeed, your very prayers have been turned into sin; and you have definitively mocked God this very day by praying for the inspiration of his Holy Spirit when you did not even believe that such a thing existed!

Needless to say, this was Charles' first, and very last, occasion for preaching there.

Though Charles chose to preach from Paul's letter to the church in Ephesus, Paul also wrote in a similar vein to the church in Rome: "Besides **this**, you know what time it is, how it is now the moment for you to **wake from sleep!**" What is the "**this**" that he is talking about? Love is the fulfillment of the Law. So, besides knowing that love is the fulfillment of the law, it is now time for us to **wake up!** For salvation is nearer to us now than when we became believers; the night is far gone, the day is near. Let us then lay aside the works of darkness and put on the armor of light; let us live honorably as in the day, not in reveling and drunkenness, not in debauchery and licentiousness, not in quarreling and jealousy. Instead, put on the Lord Jesus Christ, and make no provision for the flesh, to gratify its desires.

Coming off of a major holiday weekend where we have all gratified our desires with mountains of mashed potatoes, rivers of gravy, quarries of cranberries, and seas of stuffing, where many of us were filled with debauchery and quarreling as we competed for the best holiday shopping prices on Black Friday, where we are now more focused on Santa Claus than Jesus Christ... it is very difficult for a young **foolish** pastor like myself to preach this text without ruffling some feathers. I used to laugh when I read Charles Wesley's sermon "Awake, thou that sleepest" but now I'm beginning to understand how important it was for him to preach those words.

Today is the first Sunday of Advent, the beginning of the Christian year. Just as we came to a conclusion with Christ the King Sunday last week, today we begin by looking forward, with expectation, to the birth and arrival of our King. But here's the great paradox, even though we are looking forward to Christmas, it feels like we're stuck looking to the past. In many areas of church life this is a plague that has permeated throughout a multitude of ministries, relationships, and conversations. **We talk about where we are as a church, what we want to do, but far too many of our imaginations are trapped by the past.**

If, as Paul argues, love is the fulfillment of the law in he past, then love is most assuredly also the appropriate mode of action in the present.

Being Christian is all about love in action; not just a reflection on the past, but also a waking up to the present and the future.

For disciples of Jesus Christ, one of the hardest things to wrap our heads around is "**time.**" We are a people who regularly remember the past, in order to live into the present, while also looking forward to God's promises. We are a people rooted in time, removed from time, and unaware of God's time. Our past is constantly invading the present, and the future has already met with the present in the presence of the Holy Spirit within the faithful community.

If your head hasn't started spinning, it should be.

God's future casts a light into the present and provides the illumination of the reality by which we are all called to live. Because God has promised to come again and make all things new, a new heaven and a new earth where death will be no more, death will die, then we are called to live into God's future reality in the present. **We are called to love in order to fulfill the Law.**

What makes us unique as a people is precisely the fact that God has invaded our present with the Spirit, with his Son who walked among us, with his Word, with his sacraments, that we are a distinctive people with expectations of how the world needs to be.

For us, the time is now! Wake up!

As Christians we are not to be content with passively accepting injustices and evils in the world. Our faith demands that we reach out in love to combat the sinfulness of the world. How often do we think about our obligations to love outside of our families and our church community? **What could this world look like if we seriously considered loving all, and all means ALL, of God's creatures?**

We are creatures of the present, though we are so consumed with our pasts. Our text today encourages us to look to the future in order to know how to act. As Paul wrote elsewhere in Romans, **do not be conformed to this world, but be transformed by the renewing of your minds.** Discover newness in your lives which the future will bring.

Wake up! We are no longer burdened by living for ourselves, but we are privileged to live for God, we are a people who obey his will for our lives. That is what Paul means when he says we are to clothe ourselves in the Lord Jesus Christ. Its what he means by putting off the darkness and putting on the armor of light!

Because of Christ's redemptive act on a cross in a place called The Skull we have all been liberated from the burdens of a sinful past. We strive forth with confident steps into a future that is always bringing us closer and closer to the fulfillment of God's redemptive plan for the entirety of creation. We are here as a people of anticipation, here the first Sunday of advent, remembering while anticipating Christ's in breaking in the world in order to bring about God's kingdom on Earth.

Wake up! This moment is the eternal moment - **the now** - when the past and the future stand still, when the past ceases its going, and the future its coming. This moment is not a time that comes and goes, it is God's eternal moment, a spot of clarity amidst the ridiculous chaos of our lives.

This passage from Paul, read for us this first Sunday of Advent, deepens our understanding of the future whose coming we celebrate both in the birth and in the return of Jesus Christ.

So, how can we wake up from the sleep that we are caught up in? How can we love in such a degree so as to fulfill the law?

Love is always the essentially revolutionary action.

We love the way that Christ loved, and still loves us...

We can reach out to the lonely in our community, those who do not have a family to share this holiday season with. We can gather together in the front of the church selling Christmas trees while demonstrating Christ's love in the world through the way we reach out to those who stop by. We can participate in quilt for a cause, letting our fingers and needles and thread create a tangible sense of love for individuals in our community. We can donate money for the Children from Social Services who we have adopted for Christmas presents this year, reminding them that nothing will ever separate them from the love of God in Jesus Christ.

We can open our eyes to the injustices within our local community, and abroad, and be willing to speak out against the disparity present. We can love the unlovable, reconcile with friends and family from whom we have been separated, and we can provide a little warmth this coldest time of the year.

Our love for others, creation, and God is never just a concrete act, something that once began and continues on a course. Our love is the **Beginning**, the **Miracle**, the **Creation** in every moment of time, it sets our hearts aflame for Christ Jesus and allows us to be his body for the world.

And so, though paradoxical, what we are doing, the ways that we embody love, can be no more than **point to the victory which has occurred, does occur, and will occur in Jesus Christ.** Love directs us to the one whose very birth we now await and anticipate. Love awaits the ends of darkness which is the **Beginning of the light of the world.**

Wake up! You all know what time it is, and it is time for us to wake from our sleep. This is the beginning, another chance to start again. Whatever baggage you are carrying, whatever sin you believe is too harsh to be forgiven, whatever frustration you are dealing with in your life, today is a new beginning. We have gathered together as a community to rid ourselves of the darkness in our lives. We are here to care for one another. You are not alone. You are part of a community of faith that loves you because God loves us. **Put on the armor of light.** Prepare yourselves to be surprised by God's grace in the world.

Wake up! Put on the Lord Jesus Christ. Do not be consumed by your past, but with excited expectation live in the present and anticipate God's future for you.

This table is our Beginning. For it is here that we gather to confess our faults, receive forgiveness, reconcile with our community, and feast at Christ's table. **This place is where past, present, and future all wind themselves together.** Christ's table is the matrix of time; it is where we remember God's mighty acts, anticipate his birth and coming again, and live into the new reality of love, mercy and forgiveness.

Wake up! God is waiting for you.
Amen.

Romans 14:7-12 - Ash Wednesday Every Day

Jason Micheli

We do not live to ourselves, and we do not die to ourselves. If we live, we live to the Lord, and if we die, we die to the Lord; so then, whether we live or whether we die, we are the Lord's. For to this end Christ died and lived again, so that he might be Lord of both the dead and the living. Why do you pass judgment on your brother or sister? Or you, why do you despise your brother or sister? For we will all stand before the judgment seat of God. For it is written, "As I live, says the Lord, every knee shall bow to me, and every tongue shall give praise to God." So then, each of us will be accountable to God.

—Romans 14:7-12

If you're all caught up on *Game of Thrones*.

If, like Todd Littleton, you've already watched every episode of all 4 seasons of *Bachelorette in Paradise*.

If Donald Trump's tweets have lost some of their luster, but you're afraid to tell your friends you've turned to *Rachel Maddow*.

If you're looking for something new to watch, then I suggest you check out *Stalker*, a dark, dystopian science fiction film from the 1970s. I discovered it on *Netflix* after I'd binge-watched all 7 seasons of *Californication*.

Stalker is an allegory that tells the story of three men who journey across a post-nuclear wasteland.

Shrouded in mystery, the character called Stalker guides two other characters, who are cryptically named Writer and Professor, across the burnt out remains of a devastated civilization.

Stalker is leading them to an apocalyptic oasis called the Zone. Stalker has promised them that at the center of the Zone is a place called the Room.

In the Room, Stalker tells them, they will achieve their hearts' desires. In the Room, their dreams will come true. In the Room, you will get exactly what you truly want.

Initially, it sounds like a promise worth a journey.

Only, when they arrive at the threshold of the Room, Writer and Professor get cold feet. They're overcome with second thoughts as the frightening thought occurs to them: What if we're strangers to ourselves?

"What if I don't know what I want?" Writer and Professor, in turn, ask Stalker.

"Well," Stalker explains to them, "that's for the Room to decide. The Room reveals you, it reveals all, everything about you: what you get is not what you think you wish for but what you most deeply wish for."

At the edge of the Room, what had sounded like a dream starts to feel like a nightmare. Rather than escaping the ruins of God's apocalyptic judgement, it feels like they're about to enter into it.

Anticipation turns to dread as Writer and Professor both have an epiphany that terrifies them: What if they don't want what they think they want?

In other words, what if they're not who they think they are?

In a book about the film, critic Geoff Dyer says: "Not many people can confront the truth about themselves. If they did, they'd take an immediate and profound dislike to the person in whose skin they'd learned to sit quite comfortably for years."

Eventually, Writer and Professor run away, terrified at the prospect of standing before the Room and having their true selves laid bare.

Watching *Stalker,* this dark, dystopian sci-fi flick from the Seventies, you'd never close down *Netflix,* check it off on your queue, click off the clicker, and say to yourself *That was a happy story.*

You'd never leave a review on Rotten Tomatoes to evangelize strangers—"You've got to check out this story about the Room 'to whom all hearts are open, all desires known, and from whom no secret is hid'"

You might say it's a good story, a good flick, a good scare.

But you'd never say it was good news.

———

So how is this passage, next up in Paul's queue, "We shall all stand before the judgment seat of God," how is this good news? Judgment?

This sounds like bad news.

But the Apostle Paul left the bad news behind back in chapter 3. Back when he said that "...all are under the Power of Sin . . . there is no one righteous; not one . . . all have turned aside and stand condemned."

That was 11 chapters ago. The bad news was 11 chapters ago.

Since then, the Apostle Paul's message has been Gospel—the good news that we are justified not by anything we do but by what Christ has done.

For us.

That what matters is not our faith (or lack thereof) but Christ's faithfulness.

That what counts—what God reckons—is not our unrighteousness but Christ's righteousness.

It has been good news for 11 chapters.

Paul's apostolic announcement has been about freedom:

Freedom from the Law.

Freedom from having to do right.

Freedom from the burden of human performance.

For 11 chapters, it's been the good news of our freedom:

Freedom from judgment because, Paul told us, "...while we were yet enemies of God, God in Christ died for the ungodly."

Freedom from guilt because, Paul told us, "...Since all have sinned and fallen short of the glory of God; we are now justified by his grace as a gift."

Freedom from condemnation because, Paul promised, "...There is   therefore now NO CONDEMNATION for those who are in Christ Jesus our Lord."

———

But—

If there is no condemnation for those who are in Christ Jesus

If nothing can separate us from the love of God in Christ Jesus

If nothing we do can separate us from the love of God—

nothing:

Not our participation in persecution or war

Not our habits that lead to hardship or distress

Not our apathy that enables nakedness and peril and famine

159

If nothing we do—

If nothing we turn a blind eye to—

Can separate us from God, in whom there is now no condemnation, then how is this *good* news: "We shall all stand before the judgment seat of God?"

———

Now, I realize this is a Southern Baptist Church in a state redder than the Ayatollah, which means, chances are, this is your second favorite scripture verse after John 3.16.

But I can tell you nothing tightens the sphincters of east coast liberals quite like a verse such as this one: "We shall all stand before the judgment seat of God."

Still, even if the verse doesn't make you fret with holy fear or sweat with sudden self-awareness, even if this verse doesn't bother you, you still have to square it with the 11 chapters that have come before.

You still have to square this "...everyone will come before the judgment seat of God" with what Paul said 4 chapters earlier that "...everyone who confesses with their lips that Jesus Christ is Lord will be saved."

Which is it? Everyone will be judged? Or everyone will be saved?

How does "...all will stand before the judgement seat of God..." square with chapter 11 where Paul said that all will be saved, that God will be merciful to all.

Judgment. Mercy.

Which is it, Paul?

It can't be both/and can it?

That everyone who confesses Jesus Christ will be saved *and* everyone will stand before the judgement seat of God?

How do we square it?

Because you have to do something with it.

You can't just dismiss it as a throwaway verse because the Apostle Paul doubles down on it in verse 12: "...each of us will be held accountable before God's tribunal..."

In fact, Paul repeats it almost word-for-word to the Corinthians: "We must all *appear* before the judgment seat of God."

And you can't dismiss this verse about judgment because the Apostle Paul here sounds like Jesus everywhere—all over the Gospels, Jesus warns of the Coming Day of Judgment.

As in his final teaching before his Passion, Jesus promises that he will come again to judge the living and the dead, gathering *all* before him.

Not some.

All:

unbelievers *and* believers

unrighteous *and* righteous

the unbaptized *and* the born again

All—not some—*all*, Jesus says, will be gathered for judgement. The "saved" are not spared.

And all will be reckoned according to who fed the hungry and who gave water to the thirsty and who clothed the naked and who welcomed the immigrant.

And who did not.

"All shall stand before God for judgement," Paul says.

Just like Jesus said.

And according to Jesus's Bible that reckoning will be a refining.

A refining fire, says the prophet Malachi, where our sinful self —even if we're saved—will come under God's final judgement and the the Old Adam still in us will be burnt away.

The corrupt and petty parts of our nature will be purged and destroyed.

The greedy and the bigoted and the begrudging parts of our nature will be purged and destroyed.

The vengeful and the violent parts of our selves will be purged and destroyed.

The unforgiving and the unfaithful parts of us, the insincere and the self-righteous and the cynical—all of it from all of us will be judged and purged and forsaken forever by the God who is a refining fire.

Now, keep in mind—purgation is not damnation.

Purgation is not damnation.

But neither is it pain free. **Neither is it pain free.**

Again, how is this good news?

What's Paul doing saying this *here,* in chapter 14?

Paul left the bad news behind, back at the beginning.

But the promise that you will stand before the judgment seat of Almighty God—stripped and laid bare, all your disguises and your deceits revealed, naked wearing nothing but your true character—admit it, it sounds awful.

It doesn't sound at all like anything to which you'd say: "Amen! Me first."

———

A couple of Fridays ago, my oldest son and I milled around Charlottesville. I went to college there and now we have a house nearby.

Alexander and I walked around Charlottesville's Downtown Mall and UVA's Grounds just before the tiki torch–bearing scare mob descended from the Rotunda shouting "blood and soil" and "Jews will not replace us."

"Dad, don't make any jokes about discovering you're Jewish" Alexander whispered to me. I laughed, not sure if I should be laughing.

We saw the empty Emancipation Park snaked with metal barricades and draped with police tape.

We saw homeless men looking dazed and curious about the stage craft and street theater setting up around them.

We saw the lonely-looking white men- *boys*- wearing white polos and khaki cargo pants, whose faces, illumined by flame and fury, we'd later recognize in the *Washington Post.*

We grabbed a coffee and a soda just off the side street where Heather Heyer would be murdered the following day.

Meanwhile, some of my clergy colleagues were in an adjacent church training for nonviolent protest, learning how to lock arms, how to wash away tear gas, and how to roll over to protect your liver when you're being kicked or beaten.

There's an elementary school near the park there in Charlottesville, mostly African American kids. I used to work there in their after-school program, Monday through Friday, when I was an undergraduate.

Walking around the park with my son, I thought of Christopher Yates, the boy who had no father at home, whom I took to Long John Silvers on occasion.

Back then, he had no idea there were people in the world who looked like me who hated people like him simply because they looked like him.

Walking around that park on Friday with my son, who is not white and is growing into an ugly but necessary awareness of that fact, I thought of Christopher.

And I got angry—righteously angry—at those who would fill the park the next day.

"God damn them all," I whispered, making sure my son could hear.

————

That Sunday I led the long pastoral prayer in my congregation.

And what I prayed...I prayed about *them*.

I prayed about *them*, those whose thoughts and actions betray allegiance to the gods of bigotry.

I prayed about *them*, those whose apathy and excuses and silence tolerate hate and harm.

"Bring your judgment to them, O God," I prayed.

"Bring judgment to those who embrace terror, racism, and violence..." I beseeched.

Bring your judgment I begged.

Bring your judgment—upon *them*.

God damn them all.

It was a good prayer, I thought.

Not everyone agreed.

One man, whose mother I buried and whose kids I confirmed, fired off an email complaining about "the Stalinist regime of [my] ministry."

"Please don't use this event as an excuse to ram progressive orthodoxy down our throats. More religion and less politics!!!!!!! Please!!!!

At least he said the magic word.

I read his email and sighed and, under my breath, I said "Bless his heart," which you might not have here in Oklahoma—it's a southern euphemism for "@#$% @#$"

———

Still another worshiper took me to task for my prayer that Sunday.

Frank is in his 80s, a retired Old Testament Professor from Greenville College. He and his wife moved to my parish a few years ago to be near his daughter.

After the final Sunday service had finished and the crowd had petered away and the ushers were cleaning up the pews, Frank shuffled up to me.

He was hunched over as he always is, a knobby cane in one hand and a floppy bible in a carrying case in the other hand.

He stopped, I noticed, to face the altar wall and, with his cane in his hand, genuflected the sign of the cross, tracing it across his lips and then his chest.

Almost always Frank has nothing but unfettered praise for me, which makes him not only the President of the Jason Micheli Fan Club but its only member.

Almost always Frank has nothing but praise. Not this time.

Shaking my hand, he shook his head in a "there you go again" kind of way.

And he said: "Well, Reverend, you certainly were bold to pray for judgment on them."

I was already beaming.

Ignoring my self-satisfied smile, he added: "You just weren't nearly bold enough."

"Professor, I don't know what you mean…"

He cut me off with a "Tssskkk…." sound between his teeth.

"You only prayed for *them*. You didn't pray for *our* judgment."

"But…" I started to protest, "I was there. *We* weren't the ones with hoods or tiki torches."

"Everyone in this country is sick with judging—judging and indicting, posturing and pouring contempt and pointing the finger at someone else," he said, pointing his finger at me.

He raised his voice a little as well as his hunched-over posture: "As Christians, we're supposed to put ourselves first under God's judgment…"

"…Because we're the only ones who know not to fear the Judge…" I completed his sentence for him.

He smiled and nodded, like I'd just passed his exam.

"Christians like to say that every Sunday is a little Easter, but, every day—every day is Ash Wednesday, where we bear the judgment of God on behalf of a sinful world."

He tapped his cane on the carpet and lifted up his bible by the straps as if to say: *It's all right here if you'd just read it.*

———

And it is—all right here.

The Apostle Peter makes Paul's same point when he writes in his letter that "Judgment begins with the household of God."

The household to which Paul writes, the church in Rome, was divided against itself over issues of food and worship.

It reads in Romans like an obscure, arcane issue, but wipe the dust off their dispute and you discover it's really the same debate you see spun out all over social media, on CNN and Fox News, and across the front page of your newspaper (if you still trust them enough to read them).

It was a debate over politics and identity. It was an issue of "Us" vs. "Them."

The community in Paul's Rome had split into factions, drawn lines, created competing tribes whose divisions had calloused and calcified into contempt.

Sweep the dust off this argument and you see that the community in Paul's Rome was no different than the community in the Rome we call America.

Carnivores vs. Vegetarians.

It's different in form but not in function from Democrats vs. Republicans.

Meat-Eaters vs. Non-Meat-Eaters—it's the same dynamic as Black vs. White, Conservative vs. Progressive, Racist vs. Righteous.

Every time, in each instance—it's like Pink Floyd said; it's Us and Them.

And to them all, the Apostle Paul admonishes: "Do not judge…
for we will all stand before the Judgment Seat of God."

"Judgment *begins* with the household of God."

Pay attention now —

Paul isn't arguing (a la The Donald) that there are "many sides"
to every issue.

Paul isn't asserting that every possible practice or perspective is
permissible.

Paul most certainly isn't urging acceptance for acceptance's
sake or tolerance for tolerance's sake.

No, when Paul implores the Christians in Rome not to cast
judgment, he's instead instructing them to bear it.

To bear judgement.

Upon themselves.

When Paul reminds them that we will *all* stand before the
judgement seat of God, he's not warning them of coming
condemnation. There *is* no condemnation for those who are in Christ
Jesus.

Paul isn't preaching fire and brimstone. Paul's pointing to their
baptisms.

He's reminding them of their calling, their commissioning.

He's exhorting them to imitate Christ.

———

Frank smoothed his tie underneath his jacket but it flopped out again as
he hunched back over and shuffled out of the narthex.

He turned around a few steps later, pushed his glasses back up
his nose, tapped his cane on the carpet, and then pointed its end at me.

He said: "We talk all the time about imitating Christ, about being his
hands and feet, and doing the things Jesus did. Most of the time we're
talking about serving the poor, forgiving another, or speaking truth to
power."

"But if the most decisive thing Jesus did was become a curse for
us, taking on the burden of judgment for the guilty, then the primary
way Christians imitate Christ is by bearing judgment on behalf of the
guilty."

———

The primary way Christians imitate God-for-us is by bearing judgment for others.

Don't you see—that's how this is good news.

It's us. We're the good news.

We're the good news of God's judgment. We're the followers of Jesus Christ who, like Jesus Christ, mimic his willingness to bear the judgment of God on behalf of the guilty.

We're the good news in this word of God's judgment.

In a world sin-sick with judging and judging and judging, indicting and scapegoating and recriminating and casting blame—we're the good news God has made in the world.

Just as Jesus said, the first will be last and the last will be first.

We who are baptized and believing, we who are saved and sanctified- we who should be last under God's judgement thrust ourselves to the front of the line and, like Jesus Christ, say "Me first."

Rather than judging, we put ourselves before the Judgment Seat.

Rather than condemning and critiquing, we confess.

We bear judgment rather than cast it.

We listen to the guilty. We never stand self-righteously at a distance from them. We never forget that "there but for the grace of God" we'd be just like them, and that it is them, not us, them—the ungodly—for whom God died.

We bear judgement rather than cast it.

We confess: our own sinfulness and guilt, our own racism and violence and pettiness, our own apathy and infidelity and failures to follow.

Knowing that there have been plenty of times we've seen Jesus thirsty and not given him a drink, plenty of times we've seen Jesus an immigrant and not welcomed him.

Knowing that even when we have seen Jesus hungry and fed him that doesn't change the fact that even our good deeds, our best deeds, are like rags, for not one of us, really, is righteous and there is no distinction, really, between any of us.

We bear judgment rather than cast it.

Because we know we can come before God's Judgment Seat expecting to hear the first words spoken when God came to us: "Do not be afraid."

We're the good news in this word of God's judgment.

———

Stalker, that dark, dystopian sci-fi flick from the 1970s about a Room in which *"all hearts are open, all desires known, and from whom no secret is hid"* — it's a disturbing, unsettling, thought-provoking film.

It received hundreds of positive reviews.

It helped inspire HBO's *West World*.

The British Film Institute ranks it #29 on its list of the 50 Greatest Films of All Time.

It's a good movie.

But you'd never call it good news.

You'd never call it good news.

Not unless the cast included a few more characters, people who thrust the terrified Writer and Philosopher aside at the threshold into the Room and said to them "Me first."

80043711R00095

Made in the USA
Middletown, DE
13 July 2018